LOVE 2013

GOD, HUMANITY, ONENESS

By Jerry Alatalo

Copyright 2012 Jerry Alatalo

ISBN-13: 978-1481814676

LOVE 2013 is dedicated to humanity and all future generations. We pray that every man, woman and child on this beautiful planet will be blessed with Unconditional Love and forgiveness. Thank you for your efforts to create a new and better world for your brothers and sisters in the one family of man. Thank you for creating The New Earth.

Contents.

I believe that unarmed truth and Unconditional Love will have the final say in reality.

–Martin Luther King (1929-1968)

A. Begin.

Welcome friend. Thank you for reading these words.

The writer's original title for this work was New York Times Bestseller. New York Times Bestseller? This would have been the thought that came into the minds of many if we had kept the original title to this book. We changed the title to Love 2013 as the original displayed the writer's attraction to the fruit of action. The original title was arrived at for selfish reasons. The writer wanted to sell books and make lots of money. After thinking about the title we realized that ego was involved and decided it was best to change it.

To those who are reading these words who are not spiritually disciplined, devoted to the Creator or interested in knowledge from Creator/God, this book may not be for you.

Another reason that we considered the original title was the idea that potential readers would be more likely to investigate further and the message of the book would be found by more people. We are focused with this work on the sharing of spiritual knowledge.

One last reason for the unusual original title was to use irony to point out the sometimes humorous side of the world of books. One sees a book on cats selling like crazy and then serious books go begging for readers. One could look at other forms of media and find similar lowest common denominator products become successful financially. Today's cable television provider listings give us a large number of examples of products which have no, or next to no, value for society and humanity.

Enough said about the writer's battle with illusion.

The definition of entertain is to hold the attention of with something amusing or diverting. If you are looking to be entertained by a book you may be in the wrong place here.

If you have an interest in seeing the world become a better place for all people, all sentient beings and the entire Creation then you are very possibly on the right page. Those who are on a journey of exploration into the meaning of life and are searching for truth, may come away with something of value here.

As someone who has come to the point where writing is a full-time vocation we are hoping that you will gain from this work. Vocation is defined as a summons or strong inclination to a particular state or course of action. We have found that writing is both enjoyable and challenging. We are humbled and grateful to have an opportunity to share our thoughts and ideas with other people.

We will say at the outset here that the writer is not a guru, yogi, enlightened being, spiritual guide or adept. The writer holds no delusion of grandeur such as being a savior of any sort. He is a simple human being like every other person who finds that exploring new ideas and thoughts is somewhat invigorating. Investigating the inner worlds in search of spiritual truth is a fascinating exercise which every now and then allows one a small glimpse of our true reality.

Our writing is non-fiction and concerns the spirituality that we all share. The goals that we have created regarding the work have to do with the search for truth in this lifetime. One could say that first one must find truth for oneself and then share that truth with others. There is no guarantee that the writer's personal philosophy or interpretations will correspond with the reader's. This does not necessarily preclude the reader and writer being on the same page, so to speak, at certain points along this journey.

At the end of the day this is just fine. We are all on the journey of a lifetime and the scenery for each of us will be somewhat different. Perhaps there will be some agreements that will become apparent as this work moves along. If there are any heart to heart agreements resulting from this shared communication then we can say that the effort has been successful and worth it. Many people have a certain way of looking at things which has been passed down to them. We are confident that there are a lot of open-minded people on the Earth and that the numbers are growing by leaps and bounds.

The writer begins this work with the hope that has been present in his small number of projects thus far. The hope lies in the idea that the words will result in an improvement in the lives of people on Earth. Hope is defined as to wish for something with expectation of its fulfillment. Fulfill means to bring into actuality. So the bottom line for our effort is to bring into actuality an improvement in the lives of people on Earth.

Will the wish be granted? We shall find out but rest assured that it is the sincere wish of the writer to improve conditions on Earth for humanity. Although we like to think that we have the outlook on life illustrated in the Bryan Adams song "Eighteen Til I Die", the writer has reached the half-century mark. Any who are reading these words who have passed the half-century mark will agree (agreement number one) that time goes by unbelievably quickly.

We have come to a point in this lifetime where our tomorrows are fewer than our yesterdays.

An example of the rapid passing of the years in life occurred to the writer just before the year 2000. Perhaps a month or so before the clock struck 2000 the writer recalled twenty or so years earlier pondering where he would be in the year 2000. Around the year 1980 he had this thought and said to himself "What a silly thing to think about. The year 2000 is so far into the future that this thought is ridiculous." Then the year 2000 came upon us. It was a moment where one sensed the brevity and totality of a lifetime.

We all have these moments where we are aware of time passing and it is very interesting to say the least. The awareness of the fact that life will come to that point where we all will move on from our physical bodies is a tremendous awareness. It is fascinating to explore our thoughts surrounding the whole amazing journey that is our lifetime. The search for wisdom and knowledge concerning the reasons for our existence is a part of the journey that every soul will experience

When we look out at the world there are so many questions that are asked. The range of questions is as large as life itself. Who are we? Why are we here? What is the purpose of life? What does it all mean? Is reincarnation a reality? Is there a heaven and a hell? Where do we go when we die? Why are there wars? How is it that people suffer from poverty, disease and starvation? Is there a real possibility of eliminating human suffering?

The answer to all of these questions is Unconditional Love. God is Love.

If this work rises to the top of the New York Times Bestseller List then all of the men, women and children who read these words will become aware of the fact that Unconditional Love is the answer.

This is how it must be because this truth is undeniable.

Right now there are men, women and children coming to this truth in rapidly increasing numbers. The human race has had the opportunity to receive a gift of information-sharing over the internet that has brought much wisdom to many. As the amount of information that people have access to has increased dramatically over the last number of years, folks all over the Earth have come into contact with greater spiritual truths. The level of discernment has led to the zeroing in on important issues and the casting off of those trivial ones that have sidetracked humanity up until these days.

We are seeing the perceptions of human beings change as this worldwide process continues. The chaff is being separated from the wheat, so to speak. The chaff can be seen as anything having to do with the ego, separation between human beings, and separation from God. The wheat can be seen as all that has to do with matters of the spirit, heart and oneness. We are speaking of the

8

oneness of humanity and the oneness of humanity with God.

It is not difficult to understand that humanity is one. It is not difficult to understand that humanity and God/Creator are one. The reason that these concepts are not difficult to understand is because they are true. There is built into every human being, animal and plant this accessible truth. The only reason that these concepts are falsely perceived as difficult is because humanity has been given untruths and illusion.

When the power of Love overcomes the love of power, the world will know peace. --Sri Chinmoy Ghose (1931-2007)

We have been told that there is this group of people in another country that must be killed through warfare. They are not one with us so we must kill them.

The reason that we must kill them is that they are different and separate from us. The God that we worship is a better God than the one that they worship so this means that we must kill them. The unconditional love of our God is more powerful than the unconditional love of their God so they must die.

Those of our fighters who are seriously harmed or killed will be remembered on a day every year for their ultimate sacrifices to kill those others who are different and separate from us.

We are told that the aim of life is to accumulate as much wealth and as many material things as possible. This, we are told, is what life is all about. We are to look out for number one and reject all of the ideas of the so-called do-gooders. There are people starving to death on this planet but this is not our concern. They are

9

the others. There are people dying every day from easily curable diseases but this is not our concern. They are the others. We should watch the football game and forget about the others. Then tomorrow we can talk about the games and the reality shows and the celebrities.

There is a time for humor and light enjoyment. There is a time for seriousness and deep contemplation.

After witnessing what humanity has created on this beautiful Earth it is a wonder that every human being has not gone stark raving mad. Thank Creator/God that people all over the world are coming to their senses with the help of communications technology. Thank God that the sanity of humanity is being strengthened and nurtured through good, decent talking between folks all over the Earth. There seems to be a type of sacred timing to all that is occurring at this time.

People now have the opportunity to share ideas and thoughts with others everywhere. These ideas and thoughts that are being shared are then instantaneously shared with larger numbers of other people. As these discussions increase there are more thoughts given to solving problems and an increased effort to make the world a better place for everyone. Because Unconditional Love is the true answer to all of humanity's questions and concerns, more and more people are arriving at Unconditional Love. The words Unconditional Love are being typed at more comments sections, blogs, and chat-rooms

The words Unconditional Love are being spoken to others on fabulous technologies like Skype. People are starting their own radio programs, posting video interviews, texting, sharing on Facebook and Twitter. The communication between people is very uplifting while more people are getting their information and news from sources other than the mainstream corporate media.

Spiritual wisdom and truth is being brought into more and more people's conscious awareness. Because Love is the most powerful force in the universe we observe that the collective consciousness of humanity is coming to be more in line with that immense power of Love and oneness. The immense, immeasurable power of Love and oneness will do nothing but continue to grow stronger in the collective consciousness of humanity. For this reason every man, woman and child on Earth should be extremely optimistic about the future of life on this planet.

What is occurring on this beautiful planet at this time can be described as the second coming where the meek shall inherit the Earth. Whether the soon to occur second coming is the literal return of Christ with the ascended masters or identifies a return of the Christ consciousness to every human being is not a concern. Either way there is going to soon be a second coming. The second coming will be the result of humanity taking the steps necessary for its creation; mankind is manifesting the second coming into reality.

When the spiritual transformation takes place then every man, woman and child on Earth will experience increased joy. The transformation is already occurring for many people and as more are transformed global changes will occur at an increasingly rapid pace. After a short period of time we will be witnesses to the creation of a new world on Earth. This is nothing more and nothing less than the natural spiritual evolution of the Earth, humanity and all other inhabitants of the planet.

There will be many bestsellers written about the sacred times that we are living in. As the positive, profound spiritual changes on Earth are manifested we will experience, and many will record, the wonderful consequences which will be seen and felt by the human race. Future generations will be able to read the records from this time and stand in awe and reverence for this generation of people who accomplished the masterpiece of a new and better world.

The illusionary reality would have us provide facts, names, dates and places to prove that the spiritual evolution of humanity is happening and will result in the most magnificent series of events the world has ever seen. Intuition is defined as the act of sensing or knowing without the use of rational processes; immediate cognition. There is an intuition amongst the human race that something very, very special is about to occur. This very special something is the complete awareness and understanding by humanity of Unconditional Love, forgiveness, and oneness.

Love is the most powerful force in the universe yet cannot be seen with human eyesight. Love's immeasurable power can only be seen through use of the spiritual vision. Love is a force of spirit so it can be sensed, felt and appreciated. Spirit is defined as the vital principle or animating force within living beings and incorporeal consciousness. Incorporeal is defined as of, pertaining to, or characteristic of non-material beings. Consciousness is defined as the quality or state of being aware of an external object or something within oneself.

What we are experiencing on Earth is the restoration of balance between the world of matter and the world of spirit. These are the times that have been spoken of by the prophets. The events of a powerful spiritual nature that are about to occur are not to be feared but embraced. Our fondest wishes for the human family are going to come true. We are to be witness to the spiritual maturing of the entire human race and there is cause for rejoicing.

The nightmares that humanity has created throughout its history are coming to an end. Are you not happy and relieved when any nightmares you may have had come to an end? This is exactly how you should be feeling with regard to the planetary end of nightmares. It is obvious to human beings that certain actions on this planet are harmful and need to end. So people are no longer leaving it up to someone else to make the necessary corrections.

We are the ones we have been waiting for.

The message of humanity's positive future will be transmitted to more and more people. We have grown to appreciate writers as the work is done without regard to what possible criticisms are directed at the work. This is probably one of the largest hurdles that the creative artist must leap over if they are to remain totally honest.

If an artist makes the firm decision to be as honest as possible then the finished work will be approaching real art. We would hope that the work reflects what the writer simply had to do. This work is about Love on this beautiful planet Earth in the year 2013. It is about the true oneness of humanity. It is about the true oneness of humanity and God.

B. Love in 2013.

The title of this work is Love 2013: God, Humanity, Oneness. We predict that "Love and Oneness" will be the phrase of the year in 2013.

What is your opinion regarding the state of Love in the year 2013? Do you believe that the people on this planet Earth will experience a magnificent surge of the power of Love in the year 2013? What is the possibility that every single human being will be blessed by Unconditional Love in 2013?

We believe that there has been an amazing increase in the transformative power of Love on Earth in the recent days and months and years. Perhaps you have been sensing this phenomenon without being fully aware of what is occurring. Let us just say that you will be very happily surprised when you see with your own eyes what the absolute power of Love will mean for humanity.

Perhaps you have come to think of the writer as some sort of a Love-bomber. If one could imagine Love being a type of weapon then this would be an accurate observation. Bomb is defined as an explosive weapon detonated by impact, proximity to an object, a timing mechanism, or other means. Weapons can be used to attack or defend. If one imagines Love as a weapon of attack to defeat ignorance, desire, anger, greed and arrogance then we have a metaphor for what is occurring on Earth.

The writer admits that he is a Love-bomber. God knows that today the human race could use much more Love and a lot less of the real bombs that harm and destroy. Thankfully humanity knows this as well and is doing something about it. We may want to express our gratitude to the Creator/God and our fellow human beings for our being alive together at this time. We may want to develop our deep appreciation for being given the opportunity to witness the profound spiritual events that are being manifested on Earth.

All that we need to do to contribute to the spiritual evolution happening here is Love. This is the simple choice of Love and knowledge over fear and ignorance. Our close look at the powerful spiritual classic The Bhagavad-Gita (Gita) shortly will show us that our battle is all about defeating ignorance through the use of spiritual knowledge. With our connection to Creator/God we have the ability to defeat evil in this world. We have no doubt that the reading of the Gita will open the eyes of many to the immense potentials of humanity.

The writer would have you know that the process of writing is looked at as an exploration and a journey of discovery that is to be shared. We are cognizant that the words you are reading may influence you. So the writer is concerned that the words measure up to the divinity in all of you who read them; the divinity that is inherent in all things. All people have somewhat different paths with their multitude of varying experiences. Keep this in mind as we move along here. Just know that the writer has the reader's best interests in mind.

We have images of people's faces reading the words and we have the increasing sense of responsibility to be absolutely honest. As mentioned the writer is past the half century mark. We can imagine those readers who are younger and impressionable. Let us simply state here that the writer wishes nothing but the best for all of the readers and humanity as a whole. It is our sincerest wish that there will be nothing but positive consequences from this work.

The goal of this project is to help other people, plain and simple. We are alone here in a room with a laptop computer typing the words into the Microsoft Word document. There is a fascinating process that goes into creating a book. As one who is new to the field of writing there is the fear that your words will fail to make a difference to anyone. What happens if your family or friends or the public read the words and have a poor reading experience? What will the writer's level of embarrassment be after the work is out there for all to see?

There are writers who write because they have to. The message of the true oneness of humanity in reality will be delivered to every corner of the planet Earth. The true message that God is one with humanity and all things will be disseminated to the entire world. We are telling you that the spiritual evolution that is occurring on Earth in the year 2013 is unstoppable.

The most satisfying thing in life is to have been able to give a large part of one's self to others. –Pierre Teilhard de Chardin (1881-1955)

Humanity's awareness of Love and our oneness will grow exponentially in 2013. The evidence of this spiritual event will be seen as an increase in public identification with everything having to do with true spirituality. There will be the sensing by human beings that there is really something very powerful going on here when Love is felt. There will be Love-bombs going off in every land on the planet. We have all heard of the phrase 'going viral'. Love and oneness will be the event of 2013.

This bodes well for this generation along with future generations on this Earth. Many spiritual masters who have walked this planet have shared with humanity the wisdom of Love. There is a sense that the entire human race is accessing the wisdom of the spiritual masters. Can we imagine how positively this will effect this generation as well as all future generations? Can we sense the great changes that are on the horizon?

There is the sense that, finally, after all of the centuries of war, greed and separation humanity is going to get it right. All people will understand that we are one with each other and one with the Creator/God. Once this understanding is established the natural diminishment of harmful actions will begin. This oneness will also be with all sentient beings; oneness will include the animal and plant kingdoms as well. To put it simply there will be the true awareness that everything is God.

Mahatma Gandhi talked about the wisdom that will soon be held by every human being. He said, "This wisdom is as old as the hills." All of the true spiritual knowledge and wisdom which has been revealed throughout history is exploding at once into the human collective consciousness. Human beings in the many millions have been drawn like iron filings to a magnet when it comes to the wisdom and knowledge they are finding on their computers. The wisdom that Gandhi said was 'old as the hills' is being discovered like gold by a tremendously large amount of people.

The greatest discovery in the history of the world has been there all along. Only now humanity has the opportunity to discover for itself the gold that is ancient spiritual knowledge. It is not difficult to see why there have been so many people movements to effect change recently. The basis of all of these movements is the profound increase in spiritual wisdom that has been gained by humanity. Nothing is hidden anymore.

The power of the so-called mainstream corporate media has diminished dramatically in recent time. Many more millions of people are getting the real news elsewhere. As we mentioned earlier there is much reason for great optimism and anticipation surrounding the near future. Love and truth are flooding the people and the planet Earth in the year 2013. In the heart of every man, woman and child there has been the yearning for The New Earth where all people are kind and generous to each other.

We would say to every man, woman and child on this beautiful planet that The New Earth is being created right now. Your yearning for this new world has played a large part in the creative process that is bringing this about. We would say thank you for yearning. Your desire for a better way of living on this planet Earth is a prayer to the Creator or God or Allah or Great Spirit. Your prayers are being answered. Keep praying and yearning for a new and magnificent life for all on this Earth because it literally makes all the difference in the world.

All that humanity needs to finish this heroic task is the belief or faith that it can be accomplished.

There is no doubt that humanity now holds in its hands the faith and belief that a new and better world is being created. There is no doubt because we are seeing and

18

sensing that this creative process is alive, it is real and that the vision is correct.

There is a reason that the new and better world is coming into existence. It is because people all around this beautiful planet Earth are finding Unconditional Love where it always has lived; in our hearts. Life is Unconditional Love and Unconditional Love is life. This is an absolute, universal truth and humanity is grasping that truth.

For every one of as sentient beings there will come a day when we will transition to the other side. We all have varying thoughts about what that place is where we will go when our souls make the transition. Can we imagine all of the souls on the other side that are cheering humanity on to create the new and better world? We are talking about a world where every single man, woman and child on Earth is aware of Unconditional Love and forgiveness. Every human being on this planet will understand oneness completely and fully.

Think about this, pray about this and share this with others all around the world. Start the fire of Love and watch it consume this entire world. What higher, nobler and greater goal could there be for humanity? See the goal accomplished in your mind's eye and then through the eyes of spirit and your heart. See this world filled to overflowing with Love, forgiveness and peace. There are many on this beautiful planet making the effort to create this new and better world at this time. It is time for every heart to join together in our true reality. Our true reality is oneness.

The ultimate lesson that all of us have to learn is Unconditional Love, which includes not only others but ourselves as well. –Elisabeth Kubler-Ross (1926-2004)

Ultimate is defined as being the last in a series, process or progression. Let us look at our lives as a series or process or progression. Series is defined as a number of objects or events arranged or coming one after the other in succession. According to Elisabeth Kubler-Ross if a lifetime is a number of events in succession then the last event in our learning is the lesson of Unconditional Love. Process is defined as a series of actions, changes, or functions bringing about a result. According to Ms. Kubler-Ross if life is a series of actions, changes or functions then we will learn Unconditional Love as the result.

Progression is defined as the act of progressing; forward or onward movement. There is progression in each individual life and there is progression in the collective lives of humanity. We are all on a collision course leading to the final and ultimate lesson that we have to learn. That lesson is Unconditional Love.

We have shared the words of three extraordinary people who lived and died on this Earth. Martin Luther King, Pierre Teilhard de Chardin and Elisabeth Kubler-Ross all walked this planet.

Jesus Christ, Muhammad, Buddha, Mother Teresa and Mahatma Gandhi all walked this Earth.

What do these great spiritual messengers have in common with every single man, woman and child walking this Earth right now? The answer to the question is everything.

What does every single human being who ever walked this planet have in common with every single human

20

being walking this Earth right now? The answer is everything.

Even the least among you can do all that I have done, and greater things. —Jesus Christ

Profound is defined as penetrating or entering deeply into subjects of thought or knowledge; having deep insight or understanding; coming as if from the depths of one's being. The definition of ponder is to weigh in the mind with thoroughness and care. Take a little bit of time here to ponder the words 'even the least among you'.

Great is defined as unusually or comparatively large in size or dimensions. Now, Jesus Christ said even the least among you. His statement was without a doubt referring to everyone; from the least among us to the so-called highest among us. We are breaking down this short but tremendously profound statement by Jesus in order to discover its true importance for humanity.

Jesus said greater things. So logic tells us that Jesus was telling humanity that everyone has the capacity to do all that he did and, unusually or comparatively, in size or dimensions, **LARGER** things.

So we have learned here that Jesus told us that every man, woman and child walking this Earth can do everything that he did and even greater things. It is the truth.

It is the truth because Jesus Christ said it.

It is truth.

C. Between the Armies.

We discovered a used copy of the classic Hindu spiritual text The Bhagavad-Gita (sometimes called the Gita) years ago in a resale shop and never really got around to reading it. We got around to reading it recently and discovered that it contains powerful spiritual revelations.

It was not a "coincidence" that we discovered this powerful spiritual text.

Perhaps you may have read The Bhagavad-Gita and have been astonished with the messages of the book. For those you have not read the Gita we will first try to give you an accurate description of the text.

Perhaps we will start with a discussion of the effect that the writings of the Gita have had on notable historical figures. This may be a good way to open up to the profound possibilities and potentials that The Bhagavad-Gita offers to humanity.

Mahatma Gandhi (1869-1948) is revered in the country of India as 'The Father of the Nation'. He is an icon around the world for his use of non-violence to free the country of India from colonial rule by Britain. His profound spirituality and belief in justice have inspired the non-violence, civil rights and freedom movements around the planet. Martin Luther King, Nelson Mandela and many other leaders have been inspired by the life of Mahatma Gandhi. When Gandhi was asked to give a message to the people he would respond, "My life is my message."

Gandhi considered The Bhagavad-Gita to be his 'spiritual dictionary' and was very highly influenced by the writings. Here are some quotes of Gandhi regarding the Gita.

The Bhagavad-Gita calls on humanity to dedicate body, mind and soul to pure duty and not to become voluptuaries (a voluptuary is a person whose life is given over to luxury and sensual pleasures) at the mercy of random desires and undisciplined impulses.

When doubts haunt me, when disappointments stare me in the face, and I see not one ray of hope on the horizon, I turn to Bhagavad-Gita and find a verse to comfort me; and I immediately begin to smile in the midst of overwhelming sorrow. Those who meditate on the Gita will derive fresh joy and new meaning from it every day.

Albert Einstein (1979-1955) was a German-born theoretical physicist famous for his development of the theory of relativity. The theory of relativity caused a revolution in physics and Einstein is regarded by many as the father of modern physics. He received the 1921 Nobel Prize in Physics. He said the following about the Gita.

When I read The Bhagavad-Gita and reflect about how God created the universe everything else seems so superfluous.

(Superfluous means being beyond what is sufficient or required; excessive.)

Carl Jung (1875-1961) was a Swiss psychologist and psychiatrist. His development of analytical psychology changed the field in important ways after Jung proposed the concepts of the introverted and extroverted

23

personality, archetypes and the collective unconscious. He believed our main task was the discovery of our deep innate (possessed at birth; inborn) potential. He believed that spiritual experience was absolutely necessary for our well-being. Jung saw the psyche (the spirit or soul) as 'by nature religious' and made this the focus of his study and thought. Many viewed Jung as a mystic (one who experiences mystical union or direct communion with ultimate reality). He said the following about The Bhagavad-Gita.

The idea that man is like unto an inverted tree seems to have been current in by-gone ages. The link with Vedic (the Vedic civilization is the earliest civilization in India of which we have written records) conceptions is provided by Plato in his Timaeus in which it states... "Behold we are not an Earthly but a Heavenly plant." This correlation can be discerned by what Krishna expresses in chapter 15 of Bhagavad-Gita.

Ralph Waldo Emerson (1803-1882) was an American essayist, poet and lecturer. His essays remain vital elements of American thinking and his work has greatly influenced the poets, writers and thinkers that have come after him. Emerson said that 'the infinitude of the private man' drove his efforts and his writings. He was a mentor and friend of Henry David Thoreau. Emerson had this to say about the Gita.

The Bhagavad-Gita is an empire of thought and in its philosophical teachings Krishna has all the attributes of the full-fledged monotheistic (monotheism is the belief that there is only one God)

24

deity and at the same time the attributes of the Upanishadic (the Upanishads are a collection of philosophical texts that form the theoretical basis for the Hindu religion) absolute.

Paramahamsa Yogananda (1893-1952) was an Indian yogi and guru who introduced many people in the west to the teachings of meditation and Kriya yoga. He wrote the popular book Autobiography of a Yogi which was an aid to the introduction of Hindu/eastern spiritual practices to the western world. Steve Jobs read The Autobiography of a Yogi once a year.

In 1920 Paramhansa Yogananda founded the organization Self-Realization Fellowship. He taught Kriya yoga to help people achieve that Self-Realization.

Yogananda said, "Self-realization is the knowing-in body, mind, and soul-that we are one with the omnipresence of God, that we do not have to pray that it come to us, that we are not merely near it at all times, but that God's omnipresence is our omnipresence, and that we are just as much a part of him now as we will ever be. All we have to do is improve our knowing."

Yogananda wrote down his aims and ideals for Self-Realization Fellowship. We list these aims and ideals in this preface to our exploration of The Bhagavad-Gita.

* To disseminate among the nations knowledge of definite scientific techniques for attaining direct personal experience of God.

* To teach that the purpose of life is the evolution, through self-effort, of man's limited mortal consciousness in God consciousness; and to this end to establish Self-Realization Fellowship temples for God-communion throughout the world, and to encourage the

25

establishment of individual temples of God in the homes and hearts of men.

* To reveal the complete harmony and basic oneness of original Christianity as taught by Jesus Christ and original yoga as taught by Bhagavan Krishna; and to show that these principles of truth are the common scientific foundation of all true religions.

* To point out the one divine highway to which all paths of true religious beliefs eventually lead: the highway of daily, scientific, devotional meditation on God.

* To liberate man from his threefold suffering: physical disease, mental inharmonies, and spiritual ignorance.

* To encourage "plain living and high thinking", and to spread a spirit of brotherhood among all peoples by teaching the eternal basis of their unity: kinship with God.

* To demonstrate the superiority of mind over body, of soul over mind.

* To overcome evil by good, sorrow by joy, cruelty by kindness, ignorance by wisdom.

* To unite science and religion through realization of the unity of their underlying principles.

* To advocate cultural and spiritual understanding between East and West, and the exchange of their finest distinctive features.

* To serve mankind as one's larger self.

Paramhansa Yogananda said the following about the Bhagavad-Gita.

The Bhagavad-Gita is where God himself talks to his devotee Arjuna.

26

Sri Aurobindo (1872-1950) was an Indian nationalist, poet, guru, yogi, philosopher and freedom fighter. He wrote "Man is a transitional being. He is not final. The step from man to superman is the next approaching achievement in the Earth evolution. It is inevitable because it is at once the intention of the inner spirit and the logic of nature's process." His many writings include The Life Divine, The Synthesis of Yoga and Sivitri. Aurobindo's central vision was the evolution of human life into life divine. Sri Aurobindo created a dialectic (the art or practice of arriving at the truth by the exchange of logical arguments) mode of salvation not just for the individual man or woman but for all mankind. Aurobindo had this thought on the Gita.

Bhagavad-Gita is a true scripture of the human race, a living creation rather than a book, with a new message for every age and a new meaning for every civilization.

Aldous Huxley (1894-1963) was an English writer who has most widely known for his novel Brave New World. His essay books The Perennial Philosophy and The Doors of Perception were widely read and he was considered one of the intellectuals of his time. Aldous Huxley has a pacifist and a humanist who in later life became interested in spiritual subjects such as philosophical mysticism and parapsychology. On Bhagavad-Gita Huxley said the following.

The Bhagavad-Gita is the systematic statement of spiritual evolution of enduring value to mankind. It is one of the most clear and comprehensive summaries of perennial philosophy ever revealed; hence its enduring value is subject not only to India but to all of humanity.

Dr. Albert Schweitzer (1875-1965) received the 1952 Nobel Peace Prize for his philosophy of Reverence for Life. Schweitzer's greatest mission was to discover a universal ethical philosophy, tied to a universal reality, which would be available for all mankind. He was a German and French medical missionary, physician, philosopher, organist and theologian. Schweitzer's comments on the Gita follow.

The Bhagavad-Gita has a profound influence on the spirit of mankind by its devotion to God which is manifested by actions.

Ramanuja (1017-1117) is seen by Hindus as the leading interpreter of the dominant Vedanta school of Hindu philosophy. He was a theologian, philosopher and interpreter of spiritual texts. Ramanuja had this to say about the Bhagavad-Gita.

The Bhagavad-Gita was spoken by Lord Krishna to reveal the science of devotion to God which is the essence of all spiritual knowledge. The supreme Lord Krishna's primary purpose for descending and incarnating is relieve the world of any demoniac and negative, undesirable influences that are opposed to spiritual development, yet simultaneously it is his incomparable intention to be perpetually within reach of all humanity.

Jawaharlal Nehru (1889-1964) was an Indian statesman and politician. He was a leader with Mahatma Gandhi in the Indian independence movement and the first Prime Minister of independent India. He was the father of India's third Prime Minister Indira Gandhi. He was the grandfather of Rajiv Gandhi, India's sixth Prime Minister. Nehru spoke these words about the Gita.

The Bhagavad-Gita deals essentially with the spiritual foundation of human existence. It is a call of action to meet the obligations and duties of life; yet keeping in view the spiritual nature and grander purpose of the universe.

Rudolf Steiner (1861-1925) was an Austrian esotericist, architect, social reformer and philosopher. He based his philosophical study of knowledge on the view that "thinking is no more and no less an organ of perception than the eye or ear. Just as the eye perceives color and the ear sound, so thinking perceives ideas." Steiner early on had a philosophical basis, but later turned to a more spiritual type of study of knowledge and thought. The common goal through his process was demonstrating that there are no limits to knowledge and human thinking. He said the following about The Bhagavad-Gita.

In order to approach a creation as sublime (of high spiritual, moral or intellectual worth) as The Bhagavad-Gita with full understanding it is necessary to attune (to bring into accord, harmony, or sympathetic relationship) our soul to it.

Hermann Hesse (1877-1962) was a German-Swiss painter, novelist and poet. In 1946 he received the Nobel Prize for literature. His most widely known works include Steppenwolf, The Glass Bead Game and

Siddhartha. Each of these writings explore an individual's search for spirituality, self-knowledge and authenticity. Hesse said the following about the Gita.

The marvel of The Bhagavad-Gita is its truly beautiful revelation of life's wisdom which enables philosophy to blossom into religion.

Adi Sankara (788-820) was an Indian philosopher who is felt by many westerners to be the most brilliant personality in the history of Indian thought. Sankara's philosophy was summed up with the quote, "Brahman (supreme universal spirit) is the only truth, the spatio-temporal world is an illusion, and there is ultimately no difference between Brahman and Atman (individual self)." On the Gita Sankara said this.

From a clear knowledge of The Bhagavad-Gita all the goals of human existence become fulfilled. Bhagavad-Gita is the manifest quintessence (the pure, highly concentrated essence of a substance) of all the teachings of the Vedic scriptures.

Swami Vivekananda (1863-1902) was an Indian Hindu monk and was credited with bringing Hinduism to the status of a major world religion. He was a major figure in the introduction of the Indian philosophies of yoga and Vedanta to the western world. Vivekananda summed up Vedanta teaching by stating, "Each soul is potentially divine." Swami Vivekananda said this about The Bhagavad-Gita.

The secret of karma yoga which is to perform actions without any fruitive desires is taught by Lord Krishna in The Bhagavad-Gita.

The Bhagavad-Gita (Gita) has been one of the Hindu culture's main spiritual texts for centuries. Gita has been interpreted by many men and women through the centuries since it came to the attention of humanity. The text was believed to have been written in 200 B.C. The Gita is a philosophical poem that is set on a battlefield. The battlefield scenery of the poem has been interpreted in a number of ways including our conscience, the human body and the world.

Gita is a seven hundred verse dharmic (dharma is the principle or law that orders the universe) scripture that is part of the ancient Sanskrit Mahabharata. The scripture contains a conversation between the main characters, Prince Arjuna and his guide Krishna, on a variety of philosophical questions. Minor characters are Kuru King Dhritarashtra and his counselor Sanjaya.

Arjuna is in the chariot driven by Krishna. Arjuna is despondent as he becomes aware that relatives and beloved friends and revered teachers are the enemies that he must kill. The relatives, friends and teachers could represent negative thoughts and perceptions. Faced with a fratricidal (killing one's brother or sister) war Arjuna is dejected and turns to his charioteer Krishna for counsel on the battlefield. Krishna through the course of The Bhagavad-Gita gives wisdom to Arjuna in answering Arjuna's questions. Krishna tells Arjuna about the path of devotion and the doctrine of selfless action.

One of the many interpretations of The Bhagavad-Gita sees the battlefield as an allegory for the moral and ethical struggles of the human life. Some see the battlefield as the body, Arjuna as the conscience, Krishna as the Creator/God giving advice to our conscience and King Dhritarashstra as the demoniac choices that are an option for human beings. Others see the battlefield as the entire world, Arjuna as humanity, Krishna as Creator/God and the king as all the wrong choices we can make as humanity.

Perhaps one could see how The Bhagavad-Gita applies to every single situation that we are in at any time. As there have been many interpretations perhaps all of them are correct. Perhaps they are all correct because the Gita covers everything. Whether there is a decision which must be made on an individual basis or decisions of a collective human nature there is enough wisdom here to cover every possible situation of the physical realm.

This would be the writer's sense of The Bhagavad-Gita at this time. The wisdom and knowledge contained in the Gita is all-encompassing. After reading The Bhagavad-Gita and finding out that there are different interpretations of the text we would most strongly join with the quote from Sri Aurobindo earlier. To repeat his quote Sri Aurobindo said, **"Bhagavad-Gita is a true scripture of the human race, a living creation rather than a book, with a new message for every age and a new meaning for every civilization."**

The Bhagavad-Gita was written around 200 B.C. We agree with Sri Aurobindo that Gita is truth, it is a living creation with a new message for every age and a new meaning for every civilization.

Author's note: Your interpretation of particular verses may be different than the writer's. There is nothing wrong with that. Perhaps the writer will, upon future readings of The Bhagavad-Gita, interpret a verse the same as you did or vice versa. The text is of a type which will allow the reader to find more insights upon each subsequent reading.

We will now journey through the spiritual classic The Bhagavad-Gita. We pray that you will be profoundly blessed.

The writer's comments will be enclosed as follows: (comment…).

The Bhagavad-Gita. Chapter One.

King Dhritarashtra: Sanjaya, tell me what my sons and the sons of Pandu did when they met, wanting to battle on the field of Kuru, on the field of sacred duty?

(The field of sacred duty can be seen as the always present place in our minds and hearts where we must decide how to act in any particular life situation. It can perhaps be seen as the battle between good and evil choices.)

Sanjaya: Your son, Duryodhana, the king, seeing the Pandava forces arrayed, approached his teacher Drona and spoke in command.

"My teacher, see the great Pandava army arrayed by Drupada's son, your pupil, intent on revenge.

Here are the heroes, mighty archers equal to Bhima and Arjuna in warfare, Yuyudhana, Virata, and Drupada, your sworn foe on his great chariot.

Here too are Drishtakettu, Cetikana, and the brave king of Benares; Purujit, Kuntibhoja, and the manly king of the Shibis.

Yudhamanyu is bold, and Uttamaujas is brave; the sons of Subhadra and Draupadi all command great chariots.

Now honored priest, mark the superb men on our side as I tell you the names of my army's leaders.

They are you and Bhishma, Karna and Kripa, a victor in battles, your own son Ashvatthama, Vikarna, and the son of Somadatta.

Many other heroes also risk their lives for my sake, bearing varied weapons and skilled in the ways of war.

Guarded by Bhishma, the strength of our army is without limit; but the strength of their army, guarded by Bhima, is limited.

In all the movements of battle, you and your men, stationed according to plan, must guard Bhishma well!"

Bhishma, fiery elder of the Kurus, roared his lion's roar and blew his conch (a shell-like horn) horn, exciting Duryodhana's delight.

Conches and kettledrums, cymbals, tabors, and trumpets were sounded at once and the din of tumult arose.

(The Bhagavad-Gita is an allegorical text. The definition of allegory is the representation of abstract ideas, or principles by characters, figures or events in narrative, dramatic, or pictorial form. At this early point in the Gita we are finding a battle about to begin. We may see this battle as one we face when deciding whether or not to deceive our parents, one we face when deciding whether or not we will be unfaithful to our spouse, whether or not we will sell a financial product which we know has no value to customers, one where we must decide whether or not to start a major war on false pretenses, or spread an untrue, vicious rumor about another. The Bhagavad-Gita allegory represents an infinite number of, any and all, possible human situations and scenarios.)

Standing on their great chariot yoked with white stallions, Krishna and Arjuna, Pandu's son, sounded their divine conches.

Krishna blew Pancajanya, won from a demon; Arjuna blew Devadatta, a gift from the gods; fierce wolf-bellied Bhima blew Paundra, his great conch of the east.

Yudhishthira, Kunti's son, the king, blew Anantavijaya, conch of boundless victory; his twin brothers Nakula and Sahadeva blew conches resonant and jewel toned.

The king of Benares, a superb archer, and Shikhandin on his great chariot, Drishtadyumna, Virata, and indomitable Satyaki, all blew their conches.

Drupada, with his five grandsons, and Subhadra's strong-armed son, each in turn blew their conches, O King.

The noise tore the hearts of Dhritarashtra's sons, and tumult echoed through heaven and earth.

Arjuna, his war flag a rampant monkey, saw Dhritarashtra's sons assembled as weapons were ready to clash, and he lifted his bow.

(Arjuna is at that point we as human beings arrive at called the moment of decision.)

He told his charioteer:

"Krishna, halt my chariot between the armies!

Far enough for me to see these men who lust for war, ready to fight with me in the strain of battle.

I see men gathered here, eager to fight, bent on serving the folly of Dhritarashtra's son."

When Arjuna had spoken, Krishna halted their splendid chariot between the armies.

Facing Bhishma and Drona and all the great kings, he said, "Arjuna, see the Kuru men assembled here!"

Arjuna saw them standing there: fathers, grandfathers, teachers, uncles, brothers, sons, grandsons, and friends.

He surveyed his elders and companions in both armies, all his kinsmen assembled together.

Dejected, filled with strange pity, he said this:

"Krishna, I see my kinsmen gathered here, wanting war.

My limbs sink, my mouth is parched, my body trembles, the hair bristles on my flesh.

The magic bow slips from my hand, my skin burns, I cannot stand still, my mind reels.

I see omens of chaos, Krishna; I see no good in killing my kinsmen in battle.

Krishna, I seek no victory, or kingship or pleasures. What use to us are kingship, delights, or life itself?

We sought kingship, delights, and pleasures for the sake of those assembled to abandon their lives and fortunes in battle.

They are teachers, fathers, sons, and grandfathers, uncles, grandsons, fathers and brothers of wives, and other men of our family.

I do not want to kill them even if I am killed, Krishna; not for kingship of all three worlds, much less for the earth!

What joy is there for us, Krishna, in killing Dhritarashtra's sons? Evil will haunt us if we kill them, though their bows are drawn to kill.

Honor forbids us to kill our cousins, Dhritarashtra's sons; how can we know happiness if we kill our own kinsmen?

The greed that distorts their reason blinds them to the sin they commit in ruining the family, blinds them to the crime of betraying friends.

How can we ignore the wisdom of turning from this evil when we see the sin of family destruction, Krishna?

When the family is ruined, the timeless laws of family duty perish; and when duty is lost, chaos overwhelms the family.

In overwhelming chaos, Krishna, women of the family are corrupted; and when women are corrupted, disorder is born in society.

This discord drags the violators and the family itself to hell; for ancestors fall when rites of offering rice and water lapse.

The sins of men who violate the family create disorder in society that undermines the constant laws of caste and family duty.

Krishna, we have heard that a place in hell is reserved for men who undermine family duties.

I lament the great sin we commit when our greed for kingship and pleasures drives us to kill our kinsmen.

If Dhritarashtra's armed sons kill me in battle when I am unarmed and offer no resistance, it will be my reward."

Saying this in the time of war, Arjuna slumped into the chariot and laid down his bows and arrows, his mind tormented by grief.

(Arjuna has begun his journey of a lifetime.)

D. Never Have I Not Existed.

Chapter Two.

Sanjaya: Arjuna sat dejected, filled with pity, his sad eyes blurred by tears. Krishna gave him counsel.

Lord Krishna: Why this cowardice in time of crisis, Arjuna? The coward is ignoble (not noble in quality, character, or purpose; base or mean), shameful, foreign to the ways of heaven.

Don't yield to impotence (lacking in power, as to act effectively; helpless)! It is unnatural in you! Banish this petty weakness from your heart. Rise to the fight, Arjuna!

Arjuna: Krishna, how can I fight against Bhishma and Drona with arrows when they deserve my worship?

It is better in this world to beg for scraps of food than to eat meals smeared with the blood of elders I killed at the height of their power while their goals were still desires.

We don't know which weight is worse to bear—our conquering them or their conquering us. We will not want to live if we kill the sons of Dhritarashtra assembled before us.

The flaw of pity blights my very being; conflicting sacred duties confound my reason. I ask you to tell me decisively—which is better? I am your pupil. Teach me what I seek!

I see nothing that could drive away the grief that withers my senses; even if I won kingdoms of unrivaled wealth on earth and sovereignty over gods.

Sanjaya: Arjuna told this to Krishna—then saying, "I shall not fight," he fell silent.

Mocking him gently, Krishna gave this counsel as Arjuna sat dejected, between the two armies.

Lord Krishna: You grieve for those beyond grief, and you speak words of insight; but learned men do not grieve for the dead or the living.

Never have I not existed, nor you, nor these kings; and never in the future shall we cease to exist. (Note: Krishna is speaking of the immortality of the souls of everyone.)

Just as the embodied self enters childhood, youth, and old age, so does it enter another body; this does not confound (to cause to become confused or perplexed) a steadfast man.

(Krishna is speaking of reincarnation.)

Contacts with matter make us feel heat and cold, pleasure and pain. Arjuna, you must learn to endure fleeting things—they come and go!

When these cannot torment (great physical pain or mental anguish) a man, when suffering and joy are equal for him and he has courage, he is fit for immortality.

Nothing of nonbeing comes to be, nor does being cease to exist; the boundary between these two is seen by men who see reality.

(Krishna is saying that we were souls before we came into our body and we will be souls when we leave our body. Our souls are eternal.)

Indestructible is the presence that pervades (to be present throughout; permeates) all this; no one can destroy this unchanging reality.

(Krishna is telling Arjuna that Creator/God is in all things and that nothing can change this reality as God is impossible to destroy.)

Our bodies are known to end, but the embodied (to give a bodily form to; incarnate) self is enduring, indestructible, and immeasurable; therefore, Arjuna, fight the battle!

He who thinks this self a killer and he who thinks it killed, both fail to understand; it does not kill, nor is it killed.

It is not born, it does not die; having been, it will never not be; unborn, enduring, constant, and primordial (existing in or persisting from the beginning), it is not killed when the body is killed.

(Krishna is telling Arjuna and all who read these words the true reality is that our essence which is our soul never ends.)

Arjuna, when a man knows the self to be indestructible, enduring, unborn, unchanging, how does he kill or cause anyone to kill?

As a man discards worn-out clothes to put on new and different ones, so the embodied self discards its worn-out bodies to take on other new ones.

Weapons do not cut it, fire does not burn it, waters do not wet it, wind does not wither it.

It cannot be cut or burned; it cannot be wet or withered; it is enduring, all-pervasive, fixed, immovable, and timeless.

It is called unmanifest (the unmanifest is the Absolute, the pure and formless ground of being from which creation and manifestation arise), inconceivable, and immutable (not capable of or susceptible to change); since you know that to be so, you should not grieve!

If you think of its birth and death as ever-recurring, then too, Great Warrior, you have no cause to grieve!

Death is certain for anyone born, and birth is certain for the dead; since the cycle is inevitable, you have no cause to grieve!

Creatures are unmanifest in origin, manifest in the midst of life, and unmanifest again in the end. Since this is so, why do you lament (to express grief; mourn)?

(We enter/manifest into physical reality from the absolute and return to the absolute.)

Rarely someone sees it, rarely another speaks it, rarely anyone hears it—even hearing it, no one really knows it.

The self embodied in the body of every being is indestructible; you have no cause to grieve for all these creatures, Arjuna!

Look to your own duty; do not tremble before it; nothing is better for a warrior than a battle of sacred duty.

The doors of heaven open for warriors who rejoice to have a battle like this thrust on them by chance.

(Could this battle be what is termed 'the good fight'? Perhaps we are called upon by God to defeat all spiritual ignorance/evil in ourselves and in the world.)

If you fail to wage this war of sacred duty, you will abandon your own duty and fame only to gain evil.

People will tell of your undying shame, and for a man of honor shame is worse than death.

(Krishna is speaking about times where we see injustice and turn away and do nothing to end that injustice.)

The great chariot warriors will think you deserted in fear of battle; you will be despised by those you held in esteem.

Your enemies will slander you, scorning your skill in so many unspeakable ways—could any suffering be worse?

If you are killed, you win heaven; if you triumph, you enjoy the earth; therefore, Arjuna, stand up and resolve (to make a firm decision about) to fight the battle!

Impartial to joy and suffering, gain and loss, victory and defeat, arm yourself for the battle, lest you fall into evil. Understanding is defined in terms of philosophy; now hear it in spiritual discipline. Armed with this understanding, Arjuna, you will escape the bondage of action.

No effort in this world is lost or wasted; a fragment of sacred duty saves you from great fear.

This understanding is unique in its inner core of resolve; diffuse and pointless are the ways irresolute (unsure of how to act or proceed; undecided) men understand.

Undiscerning men who delight in the tenets of ritual lore utter florid (excessively ornate; showy) speech, proclaiming, "There is nothing else!"

Driven by desire, they strive after heaven and contrive (to plan with ingenuity or cleverness; devise) to win powers and delights, but their intricate ritual language bears only the fruit of action in rebirth.

Obsessed with powers and delights, their reason lost in words, they do not find in contemplation this understanding of inner resolve.

Arjuna, the realm of sacred lore is nature—beyond its triad of qualities, dualities, and mundane rewards, be forever lucid (mentally sound; sane or rational), alive to yourself.

For the discerning priest, all of sacred lore has no more value than a well when water flows everywhere.

Be intent on action, not on the fruits of action; avoid attraction to the fruits and attachment to inaction!

Perform actions, firm in discipline, relinquishing attachment; be impartial (treating or affecting all equally) to failure and success—this equanimity (steadiness of mind, especially under stress; calm temperament) is called discipline.

Arjuna, action is far inferior to the discipline of understanding; so seek refuge in understanding—pitiful are men drawn by fruits of actions.

Disciplined by understanding, one abandons both good and evil deeds; so arm yourself for discipline— discipline is skill in actions.

Wise men disciplined by understanding relinquish (to withdraw or retreat from; leave behind) the fruit born of action; freed from these bonds of rebirth, they reach a place beyond decay.

When your understanding passes beyond the swamp of delusion (something that is falsely or delusively believed), you will be indifferent (having no particular interest or concern) to all that is heard in sacred lore (accumulated facts, traditions, or beliefs).

When your understanding turns from sacred lore to stand fixed, immovable in contemplation (thoughtful observation or study; meditation on spiritual matters) then you will reach discipline.

(The man of discipline moves beyond traditions and beliefs to the higher way. The higher way is available to all human beings.)

Arjuna: Krishna, what defines a man deep in contemplation whose insight (the act or outcome of grasping the hidden or inner nature of things or of perceiving in an intuitive manner) and thought are sure? How would he speak? How would he sit? How would he move?

Lord Krishna: When he gives up desires in his mind, is content with the self within himself, then he is said to be a man whose insight is sure, Arjuna.

When suffering does not disturb his mind, when his craving for pleasures has vanished, when attraction, fear, and anger are gone, he is called a sage (someone venerated for the possession of wisdom, judgment, and experience) whose thought is sure.

When he shows no preference in fortune or misfortune and neither exults (to rejoice greatly; be jubilant or triumphant) nor hates, his insight is sure.

When, like a tortoise retracting its limbs, he withdraws his senses completely from sensuous (appealing to or gratifying the senses) objects, his insight is sure.

Sensuous objects fade when the embodied self abstains from food; the taste lingers, but it too fades in the vision of higher truth.

Even when a man of wisdom tries to control them, Arjuna, the bewildering (to perplex or confuse) senses attack his mind with violence.

Controlling them all, with discipline he should focus on me; when his senses are under control, his insight is sure.

Brooding (preoccupied with depressing memories or thoughts) about sensuous objects makes attachment to them grow; from attachment desire arises, from desire anger is born.

From anger comes confusion; from confusion memory lapses; from broken memory understanding is lost; from loss of understanding, he is ruined.

But a man of inner strength whose senses experience objects without attraction and hatred, in self-control, finds serenity.

In serenity, all his sorrows dissolve; his reason becomes serene (calm, peaceful, or tranquil), his understanding sure.

Without discipline, he has no understanding or inner power. Without inner power, he has no peace; and without peace where is joy?

If his mind submits to the play of the senses, they drive away insight, as wind drives a ship on water.

So, Great Warrior, when withdrawal of the senses from sense objects is complete, discernment (keenness of insight and judgment) is firm.

When it is night for all creatures, a master of restraint is awake; when they are awake, it is night for the sage who sees reality.

As the mountainous depths of the ocean are unmoved when waters rush into it, so the man unmoved when desires enter him attains a peace that eludes the man of many desires.

When he renounces all desires and acts without craving, possessiveness, or individuality, he finds peace.

This is the place of the infinite spirit; achieving it, one is freed from delusion; abiding in it even at the time of death, one finds the pure calm of infinity.

E. Men of Discipline.

Chapter Three.

Arjuna: If you think understanding is more powerful than action, why, Krishna, do you urge me to this horrific act?

You confuse my understanding with a maze of words; speak one certain truth so I may achieve what is good.

Lord Krishna: Earlier I taught the twofold basis of good in this world—for philosophers, disciplined knowledge; for men of discipline, action.

A man cannot escape the force of action by abstaining from actions; he does not attain success just by renunciation (to give up or put aside voluntarily).

No one exists for even an instant without performing action; however unwilling, every being is forced to act by the qualities of nature.

When his senses are controlled but he keeps recalling sense objects with his mind, he is a self-deluded hypocrite (a person who puts on a false appearance of virtue or religion).

When he controls his senses with his mind and engages in the discipline of action with his faculties of action, detachment sets him apart.

Perform necessary action; it is more powerful than inaction; without action you even fail to sustain your own body.

Action imprisons the world unless it is done as sacrifice; freed from attachment, Arjuna, perform action as sacrifice!

When creating living beings and sacrifice, Prajapati, the primordial creator, said:

"By sacrifice will you procreate! Let it be your wish-granting cow!

Foster the gods with this, and may they foster you; by enriching one another, you will achieve a higher good.

Enriched by sacrifice, the gods will give you the delights you desire; he is a thief who enjoys their gifts without giving to them in return."

Good men eating the remnants of sacrifice are free of any guilt, but evil men who cook for themselves eat the food of sin.

Creatures depend on food, food comes from rain, rain depends on sacrifice, and sacrifice comes from action.

Action comes from the spirit of prayer, whose source is OM, sound of the imperishable; so the pervading infinite spirit is ever present in rites of sacrifice.

He who fails to keep turning the wheel here set in motion wastes his life in sin, addicted to the senses, Arjuna.

But when a man finds delight within himself and feels inner joy and pure contentment in himself, there is nothing more to be done.

He has no stake here in deeds done or undone, nor does his purpose depend on other creatures.

Always perform with detachment any action you must do; performing action with detachment, one achieves supreme good.

(The writer has come up against the concept of attachment. He has desired profit and acclaim from the work of writing. He is aware that the producing of this work, if done with detachment, would increase the chance that the work was done with the welfare of others in the forefront. We would be honest with the reader.)

Janaka and other ancient kings attained perfection by action alone; seeing the way to preserve the world, you should act.

Whatever a leader does, the ordinary people also do. He sets the standard for the world to follow.

In the three worlds there is nothing I must do, nothing unattained to be attained, yet I engage in action.

What if I did not engage relentlessly in action? Men retrace my path at every turn, Arjuna.

These worlds would collapse if I did not perform action; I would create disorder in society, living beings would be destroyed.

As the ignorant act with attachment to actions, Arjuna, so wise men should act with detachment to preserve the world.

No wise man disturbs the understanding of ignorant men attached to action; he should inspire them, performing all actions with discipline.

Actions are all effected by the qualities of nature; but deluded by individuality, the self thinks, "I am the actor."

When he can discriminate the actions of nature's qualities and think, "The qualities depend on other qualities", he is detached.

Those deluded by the qualities of nature are attached to their actions; a man who knows this should not upset these dull men of partial knowledge.

Surrender all actions to me, and fix your reason on your inner self; without hope or possessiveness, your fever subdued, fight the battle!

Men who always follow my thought, trusting it without finding fault, are freed even by their actions.

But those who find fault and fail to follow my thought, know that they are lost fools, deluded by every bit of knowledge.

Even a man of knowledge behaves in accord with his own nature; creatures all conform to nature; what can one do to restrain them?

Attraction and hatred are poised in the object of every sense experience; a man must not fall prey to these two brigands (an outlaw or bandit, especially one of an outlaw band) lurking on his path!

Your own duty done imperfectly is better than another man's done well. It is better to die in one's own duty; another man's duty is perilous.

Arjuna: Krishna, what makes a person commit evil against his own will, as if compelled by force?

Lord Krishna: It is desire and anger, arising from nature's quality of passion; know it here as the enemy, voracious (having or marked by an insatiable appetite) and very evil!

As fire is obscured by smoke and a mirror by dirt, as an embryo is veiled by its caul, so is knowledge obscured by this.

Knowledge is obscured by the wise man's eternal enemy, which takes form as desire, an insatiable fire, Arjuna.

The senses, mind, and understanding are said to harbor desire; with these desire obscures knowledge and confounds the embodied self.

Therefore, first restrain your senses, Arjuna, then kill this evil that ruins knowledge and judgment.

Men say that the senses are superior to their objects, the mind superior to the senses, understanding superior to the mind; higher than understanding is the self.

Knowing the self beyond understanding, sustain the self with the self. Great Warrior, kill the enemy menacing you in the form of desire!

(Desire is defined as wish or long for; want, crave. Can we observe how desire has been the cause of much suffering and destruction on this Earth?)

F. Through Many Births.

Chapter Four.

Lord Krishna: I taught this undying discipline to the shining sun, first of mortals, who told it to Manu, the progenitor of man; Manu told it to the solar king Ikshvaku.

Royal sages knew this discipline, which the tradition handed down; but over the course of time it has decayed, Arjuna.

This is the ancient discipline that I have taught you today; you are my devotee and my friend, and this is the deepest mystery.

Arjuna: Your birth followed the birth of the sun; how can I comprehend that you taught it in the beginning?

Lord Krishna: I have passed through many births and so have you; I know them all, but you do not, Arjuna.

Though myself unborn, undying, the lord of creatures, I fashion nature, which is mine, and I come into being through my own magic.

Whenever sacred duty decays and chaos prevails, then, I create myself, Arjuna.

To protect men of virtue and destroy men who do evil, to set the standard of sacred duty, I appear in age after age.

He who really knows my divine birth and my action, escapes rebirth when he abandons the body and he comes to me, Arjuna.

Free from attraction, fear, and anger, filled with me, dependent on me, purified by the fire of knowledge, many come into my presence.

As they seek refuge in me, I devote myself to them; Arjuna, men retrace my path in every way.

(Can we perceive that 'in every way' refers to the many spiritual traditions on the Earth? As each are sincere efforts to retrace the path to God can we, once and for all, conclude that they are all legitimate paths that share an honest search for truth? It is time for all genuine spiritual seekers to recognize their true oneness.)

Desiring success in their actions, men sacrifice here to the gods; in the world of man success comes quickly from action.

I created mankind in four classes, different in their qualities and actions; though unchanging, I am the agent of this, the actor who never acts!

I desire no fruit of actions, and actions do not defile me; one who knows this about me is not bound by actions.

Knowing this, even ancient seekers of freedom performed action—do as these seers did in ancient times.

What is action? What is inaction? Even the poets were confused—what I shall teach you of action will free you from misfortune.

One should understand action, understand wrong action, and understand inaction too; the way of action is obscure (not clearly seen or easily distinguished).

(Karma is defined as action, bringing upon oneself inevitable results, good or bad, either in this life or in a reincarnation.)

A man who sees inaction in action and action in inaction has understanding among men, disciplined in all action he performs.

The wise say a man is learned when his plans lack constructs of desire, when his actions are burned by the fire of knowledge.

Abandoning attachment to fruits of action, always content, independent, he does nothing at all even when he engages in action.

He incurs no guilt if he has no hope, restrains his thought and himself, abandons possessions, and performs actions with his body only.

Content with whatever comes by chance, beyond dualities, free from envy, impartial to failure and success, he is not bound even when he acts.

When a man is unattached and free, his reason deep in knowledge, acting only in sacrifice, his action is wholly dissolved.

The infinite spirit is the offering, the oblation (the act of making a religious offering) it pours into infinite fire, and the infinite spirit can be reached by contemplating its infinite action.

Some men of discipline offer sacrifice only to the gods; others sacrifice with oblation in the fire of infinite spirit.

Some offer senses such as hearing in the fires of restraint; others offer sound and other objects in the fire of the senses.

Others offer all actions of the senses and all actions of breath in the fire of discipline kindled by knowledge— the mastery of one's self.

Ascetics who keep strict vows sacrifice with material objects, through penance, discipline, study of sacred lore, and knowledge.

Others sacrifice by suspending the cycle of vital breath, the flow of inhaling and exhaling, as they practice breath control.

Others restricting their food offer breaths in vital breaths; all these understand sacrifice and in sacrifice exhaust their sins.

Men who eat remnants of sacrifice attain the timeless infinite spirit; what is this world or the next for a man without sacrifice, Arjuna?

Many forms of sacrifice expand toward the infinite spirit; know that the source of them all is action, and you will be free.

Sacrifice in knowledge is better than sacrifice with material objects; the totality of all action culminates in knowledge, Arjuna.

Know it by humble submission, by asking questions, and by service; wise men who see reality will give you knowledge.

Arjuna, when you have realized this, you will not descend into delusion again; knowledge will let you see creatures within yourself and so in me.

Even if you are the most evil of all sinners, you will cross over all evil on the raft of knowledge.

(Spiritual knowledge will carry even those who have committed evil acts to the higher way. There is real hope for those who are genuinely repentant.)

Just as a flaming fire reduces wood to ashes, Arjuna, so the fire of knowledge reduces all actions to ashes.

No purifier equals knowledge, and in time the man of perfect discipline discovers this in his own spirit.

Faithful, intent, his senses subdued, he gains knowledge; gaining knowledge, he soon finds perfect peace.

(Spiritual knowledge allows us to eliminate bad karma, purify our souls and attain peace.)

An ignorant man is lost, faithless, and filled with self-doubt; a soul that harbors doubt has no joy, not in this world or the next.

Arjuna, actions do not bind a man in possession of himself, who renounces action through discipline and severs doubt with knowledge.

So sever the ignorant doubt in your heart with the sword of self-knowledge, Arjuna! Observe your discipline! Arise!

(The writer mentioned that he is not a guru or savior of any type. These verses are just as powerfully astonishing to the writer as they are to anyone who reads them.)

G. Discipline in Action.

Chapter Five.

Arjuna: Krishna, you praise renunciation of actions and then discipline; tell me with certainty which is the better of these two.

Lord Krishna: Renunciation and discipline in action both effect good beyond measure; but of the two, discipline in action surpasses renunciation of action.

The man of eternal renunciation is one who neither hates nor desires; beyond dualities, he is easily freed from bondage.

Simpletons separate philosophy and discipline, but the learned do not; applying one correctly, a man finds the fruit of both.

Men of discipline reach the same place that philosophers attain; he really sees who sees philosophy and discipline to be one.

Renunciation is difficult to attain without discipline; a sage armed with discipline soon reaches the infinite spirit.

Armed with discipline, he purifies and subdues the self, masters his senses, unites himself with the self of all creatures; even when he acts, he is not defiled.

(To the writer 'unites himself with the self of all creatures' stands out as a human perspective that is very important to understand. When a person 'unites himself with the self of all creatures' that person understands that God is in all things animate and inanimate. Can we imagine what life on Earth will be like when all have come to this understanding? This is oneness.)

Seeing, hearing, touching, smelling, eating, walking, sleeping, breathing, the disciplined man who knows reality should think, "I do nothing at all."

When talking, giving, taking, opening and closing his eyes, he keeps thinking, "It is the senses that engage the sense objects."

A man who relinquishes attachment and dedicates actions to the infinite spirit is not stained by evil, like a lotus leaf unstained by water.

Relinquishing attachment, men of discipline perform action with body, mind, understanding, and senses for the purification of the self.

Relinquishing the fruit of action, the disciplined man attains perfect peace; the undisciplined man is in bondage, attached to the fruit of his desire.

Renouncing all actions with the mind, the masterful embodied self dwells at ease in its nine-gated fortress— it neither acts nor causes action.

The lord of the world does not create agency or actions, or a union of fruits with actions; but his being unfolds into existence.

The lord does not partake of anyone's evil or good conduct; knowledge is obscured by ignorance, so people are deluded.

When ignorance is destroyed by knowledge of the self, then, like the sun, knowledge illuminates ultimate reality.

(The ultimate reality on this beautiful planet Earth will be one where ignorance has been destroyed by the light of knowledge.)

That becomes their understanding, their self, their basis, and their goal, and they reach a state beyond return, their sin dispelled by knowledge.

Learned men see with an equal eye a scholarly and dignified priest, a cow, an elephant, a dog, and even an outcaste scavenger.

Men who master the worldly world have equanimity— they exist in the infinite spirit, in its flawless equilibrium (mental or emotional balance; poise).

He should not rejoice in what he loves nor recoil from what disgusts him; secure in understanding, undeluded, knowing the infinite spirit, he abides in it.

Detached from external contacts, he discovers joy in himself; joined by discipline to the infinite spirit, the self attains inexhaustible joy.

Delights from external objects are wombs of suffering; in their beginning is their end, and no wise man delights in them.

A man able to endure the force of desire and anger before giving up his body is disciplined and joyful.

The man of discipline has joy, delight, and light within; becoming the infinite spirit, he finds the pure calm of infinity.

(The writer has not yet entered into the discipline of meditation. Evidently the effects are overwhelmingly positive. Some have experienced the stabilization of blood pressure, the reduction of stress hormones, lower levels of stress and anxiety, and increased spiritual awareness. Perhaps in the near future meditation will be practiced; first for its positive health effects. To reach that point where one actually becomes the infinite spirit would seem to be a highly valuable and important goal to strive for.)

Seers who can destroy their sins, cut through doubt, master the self, and delight in the good of all creatures attain the pure calm of infinity.

The pure calm of infinity exists for the ascetic who disarms desire and anger, controls reason, and knows the self.

He shuns external objects, fixes his gaze between his brows, and regulates his vital breaths as they pass through his nostrils.

Truly free is the sage who controls his senses, mind, and understanding, who focuses on freedom and dispels desire, fear, and anger.

Knowing me as the enjoyer of sacrifices and penances, lord of all worlds, and friend of all creatures, he finds peace.

H. What Must Be Done.

Chapter Six.

Lord Krishna: One who does what must be done without concern for the fruits is a man of renunciation and discipline, not one who shuns ritual fire and rites.

Know that discipline, Arjuna, is what men call renunciation; no man is disciplined without renouncing willful intent.

Action is the means for a sage who seeks to mature in discipline; tranquility is the means for one who is mature in discipline.

He is said to be mature in discipline when he has renounced all intention and is detached from sense objects and actions.

He should elevate himself by the self, not degrade himself; for the self is its own friend and its own worst foe.

The self is the friend of a man who masters himself through the self, but for a man without self-mastery, the self is like an enemy at war.

(Here we can see why there are such a large number of people who take drugs for depression, anxiety etc. It would seem that meditative practice would be a wise alternative. **Very important! If you want to discontinue any drug first discuss fully with your doctor. There are health risks and dangers involved when reducing or stopping the taking of various drugs.** We are our own friend or we are our own enemy. The spiritual knowledge allows us to be our own friend and not to degrade ourselves.)

The higher self of a tranquil man whose self is mastered is perfectly poised in cold or heat, joy or suffering, honor or contempt.

Self-contented in knowledge and judgment, his senses subdued, on the summit of existence, impartial to clay, stone, or gold, the man of discipline is disciplined.

He is set apart by his disinterest toward comrades, allies, enemies, neutrals, nonpartisans, foes, friends, good and even evil men.

A man of discipline should always discipline himself, remain in seclusion, isolated, his thought and self well controlled, without possessions or hope.

He should fix for himself a firm seat in a pure place, neither too high nor too low, covered in cloth, deerskin, or grass.

He should focus his mind and restrain the activity of his thought and senses; sitting on that seat, he should practice discipline for the purification of the self.

He should keep his body, head, and neck aligned, immobile, steady; he should gaze at the tip of his nose and not let his glance wander.

The self tranquil, his fear dispelled, firm in his vow of celibacy, his mind restrained, let him sit with discipline, his thought fixed on me, intent on me.

(Krishna at this point is advising discipline in the form of meditation called Kriya yoga.)

Disciplining himself, his mind controlled, a man of discipline finds peace, the pure calm that exists in me.

Gluttons have no discipline, nor the man who starves himself, nor he who sleeps excessively or suffers wakefulness.

When a man disciplines his diet and diversions, his physical actions, his sleeping and waking, discipline destroys his sorrow.

When his controlled thought rests within the self alone, without craving objects of desire, he is said to be disciplined.

"He does not waver, like a lamp sheltered from the wind" is the simile (figure of speech that directly compares two different things) recalled for a man of discipline, restrained in thought and practicing self-discipline.

When his thought ceases, checked by the exercise of discipline, he is content within the self, seeing the self through himself.

Absolute joy beyond the senses can only be grasped by understanding; when one knows it, he abides there and never wanders from this reality.

Obtaining it, he thinks there is no greater gain; abiding there, he is unmoved, even by deep suffering.

Since he knows that discipline means unbinding the bonds of suffering, he should practice discipline resolutely, without despair dulling his reason.

He should entirely relinquish desires aroused by willful intent; he should entirely control his senses with his mind.

He should gradually become tranquil, firmly controlling his understanding; focusing his mind on the self, he should think nothing.

Wherever his faltering mind unsteadily wanders, he should restrain it and bring it under self-control.

(This verse talks about the difficulty some find in stopping their thoughts during meditation. With practice it is possible.)

When his mind is tranquil, perfect joy comes to the man of discipline; his passion is calmed, he is without sin, being one with the infinite spirit.

(With tranquility of mind, we are able to commune with the Creator/God/Infinite Spirit.)

Constantly disciplining himself, free from sin, the man of discipline easily achieves perfect joy in harmony with the infinite spirit.

Arming himself with discipline, seeing everything with an equal eye, he sees the self in all creatures and all creatures in the self.

He who sees me everywhere and sees everything in me will not be lost to me, and I will not be lost to him.

 I exist in all creatures, so the disciplined man devoted to me grasps the oneness of life; wherever he is, he is in me.

(This is the understanding of the oneness of life that is being grasped by more and more of the human race at this time.)

When he sees identity in everything, whether joy or suffering, through analogy with the self, he is deemed a man of pure discipline.

Arjuna: You define this discipline by equanimity, Krishna; but in my faltering condition, I see no ground for it.

Krishna, the mind is faltering, violent, strong, and stubborn; I find it as difficult to hold as the wind.

Lord Krishna: Without doubt, the mind is unsteady and hard to hold, but practice and dispassion can restrain it, Arjuna.

In my view, discipline eludes the unrestrained self, but if he strives to master himself, a man has the means to reach it.

(When we strive we find the means to master ourselves.)

Arjuna: When a man has faith, but no ascetic will, and his mind deviates from discipline before its perfection is achieved, what way is there for him, Krishna?

Doomed by his double failure, is he not like a cloud split apart, unsettled, deluded on the path of the infinite spirit?

Krishna, only you can dispel this doubt of mine completely; there is no one but you to dispel this doubt.

Lord Krishna: Arjuna, he does not suffer doom in this world or the next; any man who acts with honor cannot go the wrong way, my friend.

(This verse shows us that any who act with honor go the right way. May this knowledge help to end the unfortunate judgments of others for their belonging to any or no particular spiritual group.)

Fallen in discipline, he reaches worlds made by his virtue, wherein he dwells for endless years, until he is reborn in a house of upright and noble men.

Or he is born in a family of disciplined men; the kind of birth in the world that is very hard to win.

There he regains a depth of understanding from his former life and strives further to perfection, Arjuna.

Carried by the force of his previous practice, a man who seeks to learn discipline passes beyond sacred lore that expresses the infinite spirit in words.

The man of discipline, striving with effort, purified of his sins, perfected through many births, finds a higher way.

(Humanity is now choosing the higher way.)

He is deemed superior to men of penance, men of knowledge, and men of action; be a man of discipline, Arjuna!

Of all the men of discipline, the faithful man devoted to me, with his inner self deep in mine, I deem most disciplined.

I. Knowledge and Judgment.

Chapter Seven.

Lord Krishna: Practice discipline in my protection, with your mind focused on me; Arjuna, hear how you can know me completely, without doubt.

I will teach you the totality of knowledge and judgment; this known, nothing else in the world need be known.

One man among thousands strives for success, and of the few who are successful, a rare one knows my reality.

My nature has eight aspects: earth, water, fire, wind, space, mind, understanding, and individuality.

This is my lower nature; know my higher nature too, the life-force that sustains this universe.

Learn that this is the womb of all creatures; I am the source of all the universe, just as I am its dissolution.

Nothing is higher than I am; Arjuna, all that exists is woven on me, like a web of pearls on thread.

I am the taste in water, Arjuna, the light in the moon and sun, OM resonant in all sacred lore, the sound in space, valor in men.

I am the pure fragrance in earth, the brilliance in fire, the life in all living creatures, the penance in ascetics.

Know me, Arjuna, as every creature's timeless seed, the understanding of intelligent men, the brilliance of fiery heroes.

Of strong men, I am strength, without the emotion of desire; in creatures I am the desire that does not impede sacred duty.

Know that nature's qualities come from me—lucidity, passion, and dark inertia; I am not in them, they are in me.

All of this universe, deluded by the qualities inherent in nature, fails to know that I am beyond them and unchanging.

Composed of nature's qualities, my divine magic is hard to escape; but those who seek refuge in me cross over this magic.

Vile, deluded sinners are the men who fail to take refuge in me; their knowledge ruined by magic, they fall prey to demonic power.

Arjuna, four types of virtuous men are devoted to me: the tormented man, the seeker of wisdom, the suppliant (asking humbly and earnestly; beseeching), and the sage.

Of these, the disciplined man of knowledge is set apart by his singular devotion; I am dear to the man of knowledge, and he is dear to me.

They are all noble, but I regard the man of knowledge to be my very self; self-disciplined, he holds me to be the highest way.

At the end of many births, the man of knowledge finds refuge in me; he is the rare great spirit who sees "Krishna is all that is."

(The concept of pantheism comes to mind. Pantheism is the doctrine that God is the transcendent reality of which the material universe and human beings are only manifestations. This is the seeing of everything as a manifestation of God.)

Robbed of knowledge by stray desires, men take refuge in other deities; observing varied rites, they are limited by their own nature.

I grant unwavering faith to any devoted man who wants to worship any form with faith.

Disciplined by that faith, he seeks the deity's favor; this secured, he gains desires that I myself grant.

But finite is the reward that comes to men of little wit; men who sacrifice to gods reach the gods; those devoted to me reach me.

Men without understanding think that I am unmanifest nature become manifest; they are ignorant of my higher existence, my pure, unchanging absolute being.

Veiled in the magic of my discipline, I elude most men; this deluded world is not aware that I am unborn and immutable.

I know all creatures that have been, that now exist, and that are yet to be; but, Arjuna, no one knows me.

All creatures are bewildered at birth by the delusion of opposing dualities that arise from desire and hatred.

But when they cease from evil and act with virtue, they devote themselves to me, firm in their vows, freed from the delusion of duality.

Trusting me, men strive for freedom from old age and death; they know the infinite spirit, its inner self and all its action.

Men who know me as its inner being, inner divinity, and inner sacrifice have disciplined their reason; they know me at the time of death.

J. Eternal and Supreme.

Chapter Eight.

Arjuna: What is the infinite spirit, Krishna? What is its inner self, its action? What is its inner being called? What is its inner divinity?

Who is within sacrifice, Krishna? How is he here in the body? And how are men of self-control to know you at the time of death?

Lord Krishna: Eternal and supreme is the infinite spirit; its inner self is called inherent being; its creative force, known as action, is the source of creatures' existence.

Its inner being is perishable existence; its inner divinity is man's spirit; I am the inner sacrifice here in your body, O Best of Mortals.

A man who dies remembering me at the time of death enters my being when he is freed from his body; of this there is no doubt.

Whatever being he remembers when he abandons the body at death, he enters, Arjuna, always existing in that being.

Therefore, at all times remember me and fight; mind and understanding fixed on me, free from doubt, you will come to me.

Disciplined through practice, his reason never straying, meditating, one reaches the supreme divine spirit of man.

One should remember man's spirit as the guide, the primordial poet, smaller than an atom, granter of all things, in form inconceivable, the color of the sun beyond darkness.

At the time of death, with the mind immovable, armed with devotion and strength of discipline, focusing vital breath between the brows, one attains the supreme divine spirit of man.

I shall teach you, in summary, about the state that scholars of sacred lore call eternal, the state ascetics enter, freed from passion, which some men seek in the celibate life.

Controlling the body's gates, keeping the mind in the heart, holding his own breath in his head, one is in disciplined concentration.

Invoking the infinite spirit as the one eternal syllable OM, remembering me as he abandons his body, he reaches the absolute way.

When he constantly remembers me, focusing his reason on me, I am easy to reach, Arjuna, for the man of enduring discipline.

Reaching me, men of great spirit do not undergo rebirth, the ephemeral (lasting only a short time) realm of suffering; they attain absolute perfection.

Even in Brahma's cosmic realm worlds evolve in incessant cycles, but a man who reaches me suffers no rebirth, Arjuna.

When they know that a day of Brahma stretches over a thousand eons, and his night ends in a thousand eons, men understand day and night.

At break of Brahma's day all things emerge from unmanifest nature; when night falls, all sink into unmanifest darkness.

Arjuna, the throng of creatures that comes to exist dissolves unwillingly at nightfall to emerge again at daybreak.

Beyond this unmanifest nature is another unmanifest existence, a timeless being that does not perish when all creatures perish.

It is called eternal unmanifest nature, what men call the highest way, the goal from which they do not return; this highest realm is mine.

It is man's highest spirit, won by singular devotion, Arjuna, in whom creatures rest and the whole universe extends.

Arjuna, I shall tell you precisely the time when men of discipline who have died suffer rebirth or escape it.

Men who know the infinite spirit reach its infinity if they die in fire, light, day, bright lunar night, the sun's six-month northward course.

In smoke, night, dark lunar night, the sun's six-month southward course, a man of discipline reaches the moon's light and returns.

(In these verses one finds the consequences of choosing either good, light and knowledge or evil, darkness and ignorance.)

These bright and dark pathways are deemed constant for the universe; by one, a man escapes rebirth; by the other, he is born again.

No man of discipline is deluded when he knows these two paths. Therefore, Arjuna, be armed in all times with discipline.

Knowing the fruit of virtue assigned to knowledge of sacred lore, to sacrifices, to penances, and to acts of charity, the man of discipline transcends all this and ascends to the place of pure beginning.

K. The Deepest Mystery.

Chapter Nine.

Lord Krishna: I will teach the deepest mystery to you since you find no fault; realizing it with knowledge and judgment, you will be free from misfortune.

This science and mystery of kings is the supreme purifier, intuitive, true to duty, joyous to perform, unchanging.

Without faith in sacred duty, men fail to reach me, Arjuna; they return to the cycle of death and rebirth.

The whole universe is pervaded by my unmanifest form; all creatures exist in me; my self quickens creatures, sustaining them without being in them.

Just as the wide-moving wind is constantly present in space, so all creatures exist in me; understand it to be so!

As an eon ends, all creatures fold into my nature, Arjuna; and I create them again as a new eon begins.

Gathering in my own nature, again and again I freely create this whole throng of creatures, helpless in the force of my nature.

These actions do not bind me, since I remain detached in all my actions, Arjuna, as if I stood apart from them.

Nature, with me as her inner eye, bears animate and inanimate beings; and by reason of this, Arjuna, the universe continues to turn.

Deluded men despise me in the human form I have assumed, ignorant of my higher existence as the great lord of creatures.

Reason warped, hope, action, and knowledge wasted, they fall prey to a seductive fiendish, demonic nature.

In single-minded dedication, great souls devote themselves to my divine nature, knowing me as unchanging, the origin of creatures.

Always glorifying me, striving, firm in their vows, paying me homage (special honor or respect shown or expressed publicly) with devotion, they worship me, always disciplined.

Sacrificing through knowledge, others worship my universal presence in its unity and in its many different aspects.

I am the rite, the sacrifice, the libation for the dead, the healing herb, the sacred hymn, the clarified butter, the fire, the oblation.

I am the universal father, mother, granter of all, grandfather, object of knowledge, purifier, holy syllable OM, threefold sacred lore.

I am the way, sustainer, lord, witness, shelter, refuge, friend, source, dissolution, stability, treasure, and unchanging seed.

I am the heat that withholds and sends down the rains; I am immortality and death; both being and nonbeing am I.

Men learned in sacred lore, Soma (drink of immortality) drinkers, their sins absolved, worship me with sacrifices, seeking to win heaven. Reaching the holy world of Indra, king of the gods, they savor the heavenly delights of the gods in the celestial sphere.

When they have long enjoyed the world of heaven and their merit is exhausted, they enter the mortal world; following the duties ordained in sacred lore, desiring desires, they obtain what is transient (passing quickly into and out of existence).

Men who worship me, thinking solely of me, always disciplined, win the reward I secure.

When devoted men sacrifice to other deities with faith, they sacrifice to me, Arjuna, however aberrant (straying from the right way) the rites.

I am the enjoyer and the lord of all sacrifices; they do not know me in reality, and so they fail.

Votaries (devotees) of the gods go to the gods, ancestor-worshippers go to the ancestors, those who propitiate (to gain the favor or goodwill of) ghosts go to them, and my worshippers go to me.

The leaf or flower or fruit or water that he offers with devotion, I take from the man of self-restraint in response to his devotion.

Whatever you do—what you take, what you offer, what you give, what penances you perform—do as an offering to me, Arjuna!

You will be freed from the bonds of action, from the fruit of fortune and misfortune; armed with the discipline of renunciation, your self liberated, you will join me.

I am impartial to all creatures, and no one is hateful or dear to me; but men devoted to me are in me, and I am within them.

If he is devoted solely to me, even a violent criminal must be deemed a man of virtue, for his resolve is right.

His spirit quickens to sacred duty, and he finds eternal peace; Arjuna, know that no one devoted to me is lost.

If they rely on me, Arjuna, women, commoners, men of low rank, even men born in the womb of evil, reach the highest way.

How easy it is then for holy priests and devoted royal sages—in this transient world of sorrow, devote yourself to me!

Keep me in your mind and devotion, sacrifice to me, bow to me, discipline your self toward me, and you will reach me!

("But seek first his kingdom and his righteousness, and all these things shall be yours as well." Matthew 6:33)

L. Great Warrior.

Chapter Ten.

Lord Krishna: Great Warrior, again hear my word in its supreme form; desiring your good, I speak to deepen your love.

Neither the multitude of gods nor great sages know my origin, for I am the source of all the gods and great sages.

A mortal who knows me as the unborn, beginningless great lord of the worlds is freed from all delusions and all evils.

Understanding, knowledge, nondelusion, patience, truth, control, tranquility, joy, suffering, being, nonbeing, fear, and fearlessness...

Nonviolence, equanimity, contentment, penance, charity, glory, disgrace, these diverse attitudes of creatures' arise from me.

The seven ancient great sages and the four ancestors of man are mind-born aspects of me; their progeny (descendants) fills the world.

The man who in reality knows my power and my discipline is armed with unwavering discipline; in this there is no doubt.

I am the source of everything, and everything proceeds from me; filled with my existence, wise men realizing this are devoted to me.

Thinking and living deep in me, they enlighten one another by constantly telling of me for their own joy and delight.

To men of enduring discipline, devoted to me with affection, I give the discipline of understanding by which they come to me.

Dwelling compassionately deep in the self, I dispel darkness born of ignorance with the radiant light of knowledge.

Arjuna: You are supreme, the infinite spirit, the highest abode, sublime (supreme) purifier, man's spirit, eternal, divine, the primordial god, unborn, omnipotent. So the ancient seers spoke of you, as did the epic poet Vyasa and the bards who sang for gods, ancestors, and men; and now you tell me yourself.

Lord Krishna, I realize the truth of all you tell me; neither gods nor demons know your manifest nature.

You know yourself through the self, Krishna; Supreme among Men, Sustainer and Lord of Creatures, God of Gods, Master of the Universe!

Tell me without reserve the divine powers of your self, powers by which you pervade these worlds.

Lord of Discipline, how can I know you as I meditate on you—in what diverse aspects can I think of you, Krishna?

Recount in full extent the discipline and power of your self; Krishna, I can never hear enough of your immortal speech.

Lord Krishna: Listen, Arjuna, as I recount for you in essence the divine powers of my self; endless is my extent.

I am the self abiding in the heart of all creatures; I am their beginning, their middle, and their end.

I am Vishnu striding among sun gods, the radiant sun among lights; I am lightning among wind gods, the moon among the stars.

I am the song in sacred lore; I am Indra, the king of the gods; I am the mind of the senses, the consciousness of creatures.

I am gracious Shiva among howling storm gods, the lord of wealth among demigods and demons, fire blazing among the bright gods; I am golden Meru towering over the mountains.

Arjuna, know me as the gods teacher, chief of the household priests; I am the god of war among generals; I am the ocean of lakes.

I am Bhrigu, priest of the great seers; of words, I am the eternal syllable OM, the prayer of sacrifices; I am Himalaya, the measure of what endures.

Among trees, I am the sacred fig-tree; I am chief of the divine sages, leader of the celestial musicians, the recluse philosopher among saints.

Among horses, know me as the immortal stallion born from the sea of elixir; among elephants, the divine king's mount; among men, the king.

I am the thunderbolt among weapons, among cattle, the magical wish-granting cow; I am the procreative god of love, the king of the snakes.

I am the endless cosmic serpent, the lord of all sea creatures; I am the chief of the ancestral fathers; of restraints, I am death.

I am the pious (reverence and devotion to divine worship) son of demons; of measures, I am time; I am the lion among wild animals, the eagle among birds.

I am the purifying wind, the warrior Rama bearing arms, the sea-monster crocodile, the flowing river Ganges.

I am the beginning, the middle, and the end of creations, Arjuna; of sciences, I am the science of the self; I am the dispute of orators.

I am the vowel *a* of the syllabary, the pairing of words in a compound; I am indestructible time, the creator facing everywhere at once.

I am death the destroyer of all, the source of what will be, the feminine powers: fame, fortune, speech, memory, intelligence, resolve, patience.

I am the great ritual chant, the meter of sacred song, the most sacred month in the year, the spring blooming with flowers.

I am the dice game of gamblers, the brilliance of fiery heroes. I am victory and resolve, the lucidity of lucid men.

I am Krishna among my mighty kinsmen; I am Arjuna among the Pandava princes; I am the epic poet Vyasa among sages, the inspired singer among bards.

I am the scepter of rulers, the morality of ambitious men; I am the silence of mysteries, what men of knowledge know.

Arjuna, I am the seed of all creatures; nothing animate or inanimate could exist without me.

Fiery Hero, endless are my divine powers—of my power's extent I have barely hinted.

Whatever is powerful, lucid, splendid, or invulnerable has its source in a fragment of my brilliance.

What use is so much knowledge to you, Arjuna? I stand sustaining this entire world with a fragment of my being.

(God is in all things. Humanity is discovering the Creator/God that is present in every man, woman and child.)

M. Here as One.

Chapter Eleven.

Arjuna: To favor me you revealed the deepest mystery of the self, and by your words my delusion is dispelled.

I heard from you in detail how creatures come to be and die, Krishna, and about the self in its immutable greatness.

Just as you have described yourself, I wish to see your form in all its majesty, Krishna, Supreme among Men.

If you think I can see it, reveal to me your immutable self, Krishna, Lord of Discipline.

Lord Krishna: Arjuna, see my forms in hundreds and thousands; diverse, divine, of many colors and shapes.

See the sun gods, gods of light, howling storm gods, twin gods of dawn, the gods of wind, Arjuna, wondrous forms not seen before.

Arjuna, see all the universe, animate and inanimate, and whatever else you wish to see; all stands here as one in my body.

But you cannot see me with your own eye; I will give you a divine eye to see the majesty of my discipline.

Sanjaya; O King, saying this, Krishna, the great lord of discipline, revealed to Arjuna the true majesty of his form.

It was a multiform, wondrous vision, with countless mouths and eyes and celestial ornaments, brandishing many divine weapons.

Everywhere was boundless divinity containing all astonishing things, wearing divine garlands and garments, anointed with divine perfume.

If the light of a thousand suns were to rise in the sky at once, it would be like the light of that great spirit.

(A woman who had a near death experience described, "The light exploded under me and went out in every direction. The light was infinite. There was nothing else to this light but Love.")

Arjuna saw all the universe in its many ways and parts, standing as one in the body of the god of gods.

(Another woman who had a near death experience said, "…the light is so much more than the sun. The light is alive with a feeling of Love and compassion; it contains a million fragments of all the souls that will or ever will be in a Love that is so overpowering and otherworldly.")

Then filled with amazement, his hair bristling on his flesh, Arjuna bowed his head to the god, joined his hands in homage, and spoke.

Arjuna: I see the gods in your body, O God, and hordes of varied creatures: Brahma, the cosmic creator, on his lotus throne, all the seers and celestial serpents.

I see your boundless form everywhere, the countless arms, bellies, mouths, and eyes; Lord of All, I see no end, or middle or beginning to your totality.

I see you blazing through the fiery rays of your crown, mace, and discus, hard to behold in the burning light of fire and sun that surrounds your measureless presence.

You are to be known as supreme eternity, the deepest treasure of all that is, the immutable guardian of enduring sacred duty; I think you are man's timeless spirit.

I see no beginning or middle or end to you; only boundless strength in your endless arms, the moon and

84

sun in your eyes, your mouths of consuming flames, your own brilliance scorching this universe.

You alone fill the space between heaven and earth and all the directions; seeing this awesome, terrible form of yours, Great Soul, the three worlds tremble.

Throngs (a large group of people; multitude) of gods enter you, some in their terror make gestures of homage to invoke you; throngs of great sages and saints hail you and praise you in resounding hymns.

Howling storm gods, sun gods, bright gods, and gods of ritual, gods of the universe, twin gods of dawn, wind gods, vapor-drinking ghosts, throngs of celestial musicians, demigods, demons, and saints, all gaze at you amazed.

Seeing the many mouths and eyes of your great form, its many arms, thighs, feet, bellies, and fangs, the worlds tremble and so do I.

Vishnu, seeing you brush the clouds with flames of countless colors, your mouths agape, your huge eyes blazing, my inner self quakes and I find no resolve or tranquility.

Seeing the fangs protruding from your mouths like the fires of time, I lose my bearings and I find no refuge; be gracious, Lord of Gods, Shelter of the Universe.

All those sons of the blind king Dhritarashtra come accompanied by troops of kings, by the generals Bhishma, Drona, Karna, and by our battle leaders.

Rushing through your fangs into grim mouths, some are dangling from heads crushed between your teeth.

As roiling river waters stream headlong toward the sea, so do these human heroes enter into your blazing mouths.

As moths in the frenzy of destruction fly into a blazing flame, worlds in the frenzy of destruction enter your mouths.

You lick at the worlds around you, devouring them with flaming mouths; and your terrible fires scorch the entire universe, filling it, Vishnu, with violent rays.

Tell me—who are you in this terrible form? Homage to you, Best of Gods! Be gracious! I want to know you as you are in your beginning. I do not comprehend the course of your ways.

Lord Krishna: I am time grown old, creating world destruction, set in motion to annihilate the worlds; even without you, all these warriors arrayed in hostile ranks will cease to exist.

Therefore, arise and win glory! Conquer your foes and fulfill your kingship! They are already killed by me. Be just my instrument, the archer by my side!

(We are able to defeat our enemies of ignorance, desire, attachment, anger, individuality and ego. As we connect with discipline to God within we gain the power to overcome.)

Drona, Bhishma, Jayadratha, and Karna, and all the other battle heroes, are killed by me. Kill them without wavering; fight, and you will conquer your foes in battle!

Sanjaya: Hearing Krishna's words, Arjuna trembled under his crown, and he joined his hands in reverent homage; terrified of his fear, he bowed to Krishna and stammered in reply.

Arjuna: Krishna, the universe responds with joy and rapture to your glory, terrified demons flee in far directions, and saints throng to bow in homage.

86

Why should they not bow in homage to you, Great Soul, Original Creator, more venerable than the creator Brahma? Boundless Lord of Gods, Shelter of All That Is, you are eternity, being, nonbeing, and beyond.

You are the original god, the primordial spirit of man, the deepest treasure of all that is, knower and what is to be known, the supreme abode; you pervade the universe, Lord of Boundless Form.

You are the gods of wind, death, fire, and water; the moon; the lord of life; and the great ancestor. Homage to you, a thousand times homage! I bow in homage to you again and yet again.

I bow in homage before you and behind you; I bow everywhere to your omnipresence! You have boundless strength and limitless force; you fulfill all that you are.

Thinking you a friend, I boldly said, "Welcome, Krishna! Welcome, cousin, friend!" From negligence or through Love, I failed to know your greatness.

If in jest I offended you, alone or publicly, at sport, rest, sitting, or at meals, I beg your patience, unfathomable Krishna.

You are the father of the world of animate and inanimate things, its venerable teacher, most worthy of worship, without equal. Where in all three worlds is another to match your extraordinary power?

I bow to you, I prostrate my body, I beg you to be gracious, Worshipful Lord—as a father to a son, a friend to a friend, a lover to a beloved, O God, bear with me.

I am thrilled, and yet my mind trembles with fear at seeing what has not been seen before. Show me, God, the form I know—be gracious, Lord of Gods, Shelter of the World.

I want to see you as before, with your crown and mace, and the discus in your hand. O Thousand-Armed God, assume the four-armed form embodied in your totality.

Lord Krishna: To grace you, Arjuna, I revealed through self-discipline my higher form, which no one but you has ever beheld—brilliant, total, boundless, primal.

Not through sacred lore or sacrificial ritual or study or charity, not by rites or by terrible penances can I be seen in this form in the world of men by anyone but you, Great Hero.

Do not tremble or suffer confusion from seeing my horrific form; your fear dispelled, your mind full of Love, see my form again as it was.

Sanjaya: Saying this to Arjuna, Krishna once more revealed his intimate form; resuming his gentle body, the great spirit let the terrified hero regain his breath.

Arjuna: Seeing your gentle human form, Krishna, I recover my own nature, and my reason is restored.

Lord Krishna: This form you have seen is rarely revealed; the gods are constantly craving for a vision of this form.

Not through sacred lore, penances, charity, or sacrificial rites can I be seen in the form that you saw me.

By devotion alone can I, as I really am, be known and seen and entered into, Arjuna.

Acting only for me, intent on me, free from attachment, hostile to no creature, Arjuna, a man of devotion comes to me.

N. Welfare of All.

Chapter Twelve.

Arjuna: Who best knows discipline: men who worship you with devotion, ever disciplined, or men who worship the imperishable, unmanifest?

Lord Krishna: I deem most disciplined men of enduring discipline who worships me with true faith, entrusting their minds to me.

Men reach me too who worship what is imperishable, ineffable, unmanifest, omnipresent, inconceivable, immutable at the summit of existence.

Mastering their senses, with equanimity toward everything, they reach me, rejoicing in the welfare of all creatures.

It is more arduous when their reason clings to my unmanifest nature; for men constrained by bodies, the unmanifest way is hard to attain.

But men intent on me renounce all actions to me and worship me, meditating with singular discipline.

When they entrust reason to me, Arjuna, I soon arise to rescue them from the ocean of death and rebirth.

Focus your mind on me, let your understanding enter me; then you will dwell in me without doubt.

If you cannot concentrate your thought firmly on me, then seek to reach me, Arjuna, by discipline in practice.

Even if you fail in practice, dedicate yourself to action; performing actions for my sake, you will achieve success.

If you are powerless to do even this, rely on my discipline, be self-controlled, and reject all fruit of action.

Knowledge is better than practice, meditation better than knowledge, rejecting fruits of action is better still—it brings peace.

One who bears hate for no creature is friendly, compassionate, unselfish, free of individuality, patient, the same in suffering and joy.

Content always, disciplined, self-controlled, firm in his resolve, his mind and understanding dedicated to me, devoted to me, he is dear to me.

Disinterested, pure, skilled, indifferent, untroubled, relinquishing all involvements, devoted to me, he is dear to me.

He does not rejoice or hate, grieve or feel desire; relinquishing fortune and misfortune, the man of devotion is dear to me.

Impartial to foe and friend, honor and contempt, cold and heat, joy and suffering, he is free from attachment.

Neutral to blame and praise, silent, content with his fate, unsheltered, firm in thought, the man of devotion is dear to me.

Even more dear to me are devotees who cherish this elixir of sacred duty as I have taught it, intent on me in their faith.

O. This Body is the Field.

Chapter Thirteen.

Lord Krishna: The field denotes this body, and wise men call one who knows it the field-knower.

Know me as the field-knower in all fields—what I deem to be knowledge is knowledge of the field and its knower.

Hear from me in summary what the field is in its character and changes, and of the field-knower's power.

Ancient seers have sung of this in many ways, with varied meters and with aphorisms (a brief statement of a principle) on the infinite spirit laced with logical arguments.

The field contains the great elements, individuality, understanding, unmanifest nature, the eleven senses, and the five sense realms.

Longing, hatred, happiness, suffering, bodily form, consciousness, resolve, thus is this field with its changes defined in summary.

Knowledge means humility, sincerity, non-violence, patience, honesty, reverence for one's teacher, purity, stability, self-restraint.

Dispassion toward sense objects and absence of individuality, seeing the defects in birth, death, old age, sickness, and suffering;

Detachment, uninvolvement with sons, wife, and home, constant equanimity in fulfillment and frustration;

Unwavering devotion to me with singular discipline; retreating to a place of solitude, avoiding worldly affairs;

Persistence in knowing the self, seeing what knowledge of reality means—all this is called knowledge, the opposite is ignorance.

I shall teach you what is to be known; for knowing it, one attains immortality; it is called the supreme infinite spirit, beginningless, neither being or nonbeing.

Its hands and feet reach everywhere; its head and face see in every direction; hearing everything, it remains in the world, enveloping all.

Lacking all the sense organs, it shines in their qualities; unattached, it supports everything; without qualities, it enjoys them.

Outside and within all creatures, inanimate but still animate, too subtle to be known, it is far distant, yet near.

Undivided, it seems divided among creatures; understood as their sustainer, it devours and creates them.

The light of lights beyond darkness it is called; knowledge attained by knowledge, fixed in the heart of everyone.

So, in summary I have explained the field and knowledge of it; a man devoted to me, knowing this, enters into my being.

Know that both nature and man's spirit have no beginning, that qualities and changes have their origin in nature.

For its agency in producing effects, nature is called a cause; in the experience of joy and suffering, man's spirit is called a cause.

Man's spirit is set in nature, experiencing the qualities born of nature; its attachment to the qualities causes births in the wombs of good and evil.

Witness, consenter, sustainer, enjoyer—the great lord is called the highest self, man's true spirit in this body.

Knowing nature and the spirit of man, as well as the qualities of nature, one is not born again—no matter how one now exists.

By meditating on the self, some men see the self through the self; others see by philosophical discipline; others by the discipline of action.

Others, despite their ignorance, revere what they hear from other men; they too cross beyond death, intent on what they hear.

Arjuna, know that anything inanimate or alive with motion is born from the union of the field and its knower.

He really sees who sees the highest lord standing equal among all creatures, undecaying amid destruction.

Seeing the lord standing the same everywhere, the self cannot injure itself and goes the highest way.

He really sees who sees that all actions are performed by nature alone and that the self is not the actor.

When he perceives the unity existing in separate creatures and how they expand from unity, he attains the infinite spirit.

(This is the perception of oneness; understanding that Creator/God is in all things and that in harming others we only harm ourselves.)

Beginningless, without qualities, the supreme self is unchanging; even abiding in a body, Arjuna, it does not act, nor is it defiled.

Just as all-pervading space remains unsullied (not stained, soiled, or tarnished) in its subtlety, so the self in every body remains unsullied.

Just as one sun illumines this entire world, so the master of the field illumines the entire field.

They reach the highest state who with the eye of knowledge knows the boundary between the knower and its field, and the freedom creatures have from nature.

P. Origin of All.

Chapter Fourteen.

Lord Krishna: I shall teach you still more of the farthest knowledge one can know; knowing it, all the sages have reached perfection.

Resorting to this knowledge, they follow the ways of my sacred duty; in creation they are not reborn, in dissolution (decay, death) they suffer no sorrow.

My womb is the great infinite spirit; in it I place the embryo, and from this, Arjuna, comes the origin of all creatures.

The infinite spirit is the great womb of all forms that come to be in all wombs, and I am the seed-giving father.

Lucidity, passion, dark inertia—these qualities inherent in nature bind the unchanging embodied self in the body.

Lucidity, being untainted, is luminous and without decay; it binds one with attachment to joy and knowledge, Arjuna.

Know that passion is emotional, born of craving and attachment; it binds the embodied self with attachment to action.

Know dark inertia born of ignorance as the delusion of every embodied self; it binds one with negligence, indolence, and sleep, Arjuna.

Lucidity addicts one to joy, and passion to actions, but dark inertia obscures knowledge and addicts one to negligence.

When lucidity dominates passion and inertia, it thrives; and likewise when passion or inertia dominates the other two.

When the light of knowledge shines in all the body's senses then one knows that lucidity prevails.

When passion increases, Arjuna, greed and activity, involvement in actions, disquiet, and longing arise.

When dark inertia increase, obscurity and inactivity, negligence and delusion arise.

When lucidity prevails, the self whose body dies enters the untainted worlds of those who know reality.

When he dies in passion, he is born among lovers of action; so when he dies in dark inertia, he is born into wombs of folly.

The fruit of good conduct is pure and untainted they say, but suffering is the fruit of passion, ignorance the fruit of dark inertia.

From lucidity knowledge is born; from passion comes greed; from dark inertia come negligence, delusion, and ignorance.

(It would be the wisest choice to strive for lucidity.)

Men who are lucid go upward; men of passion stay in between; men of dark inertia, caught in vile ways, sink low.

When a man of vision sees nature's qualities as the agent of action and knows what lies beyond, he enters into my being.

Transcending the three qualities that are the body's source, the self achieves immortality, freed from the sorrows of birth, death, and old age.

Arjuna: Lord, what signs mark a man who passes beyond the three qualities? What does he do to cross beyond these qualities?

Krishna: He does not dislike light or activity or delusion; when they cease to exist he does not desire them.

He remains disinterested, unmoved by qualities of nature; he never wavers, knowing that only qualities are in motion.

Self-reliant, impartial to suffering and joy, to clay, stone, or gold, the resolute man is the same to foe and friend, to blame and praise.

The same in honor and disgrace, to ally and enemy, a man who abandons involvements transcends the qualities of nature.

One who serves me faithfully, with discipline of devotion, transcends the qualities of nature and shares in the infinite spirit.

I am the infinite spirit's foundation, immortal and immutable, the basis of eternal sacred duty and of perfect joy.

Q. The Tree of Life.

Chapter Fifteen.

Lord Krishna: Roots in the air, branches below, the tree of life is unchanging, they say; its leaves are hymns, and he who knows it knows sacred lore.

Its branches stretch below and above, nourished by nature's qualities, budding with sense objects; aerial roots tangled in actions reach downward into the world of men.

Its form is unknown here in the world; unknown are its end, its beginning, its extent; cut down this tree that has such deep roots with the sharp ax of detachment.

Then search to find the realm that one enters without returning: "I seek the refuge in the original spirit of man, from which primordial activity extended."

Without pride or delusion, the fault of attachment overcome, intent on the self within, their desires extinguished, freed from dualities, from joy and suffering, undeluded men reach that realm beyond change.

Neither sun nor moon nor fire illumines my highest abode—once there, they do not return.

A fragment of me in the living world is the timeless essence of life; it draws out the senses and the mind inherent in nature.

When the lord takes on a body and then leaves it, he carries these along, like the wind bearing scents from earth.

Governing, hearing, sight, touch, taste, smell, and thought, he savors objects of the senses.

Deluded men do not perceive him in departure or presence or enjoyment of nature's qualities; but the eyes of knowledge see him.

Men of discipline who strive see him present within themselves; but without self-mastery and reason, even those who strive fail to see.

(Creator/God is inside of us all. We must attain self-mastery to see God within.)

Know that my brilliance, flaming in the sun, in the moon, and in fire, illumines the whole universe.

I penetrate the earth and sustain creatures by my strength; becoming Soma, the liquid of moonlight, I nurture all healing herbs.

I am the universal fire within the body of living beings; I work with the flow of vital breath to digest the foods that men consume.

I dwell deep in the heart of everyone; memory, knowledge, and reasoning come from me; I am the object to be known through all sacred lore; and I am its knower, the creator of its final truth.

There is a double spirit of man in the world, transient and eternal—transient in all creatures, eternal at the summit of existence.

(Our physical body is manifested here for a short time. Depending on our spiritual development we will be reborn or escape rebirth.)

Other is the supreme spirit of man, called the supreme self, the immutable lord who enters and sustains the three worlds.

Since I transcend what is transient and I am higher than the eternal, I am known as the supreme spirit of man in the world and in sacred lore.

Whoever knows me without delusion as the supreme spirit of man knows all there is, Arjuna—he devotes his whole being to me.

Arjuna, thus I have taught this most secret tradition; realizing it, one has understanding and his purpose is fulfilled.

R. Divine or Demonic.

Chapter Sixteen.

Lord Krishna: Fearlessness, purity, determination in the discipline of knowledge, charity, self-control, sacrifice, study of sacred lore, penance, honesty;

Non-violence, truth, absence of anger, disengagement, peace, loyalty, compassion for creatures, lack of greed, gentleness, modesty, reliability;

Brilliance, patience, resolve, clarity, absence of envy and of pride; these characterize a man born with divine traits.

Hypocrisy, arrogance, vanity, anger, harshness, ignorance; these characterize a man born with demonic traits.

The divine traits lead to freedom, the demonic lead to bondage; do not despair, Arjuna; you were born with the divine.

All creatures in the world are either divine or demonic; I described the divine at length; hear what I say about the demonic.

Demonic men cannot comprehend activity and rest; there exists no clarity, no morality, no truth in them.

They say that the world has no truth, no basis, no god, that no power of mutual dependence is its cause, but only desire.

Mired in this view, lost to themselves with their meager understanding, these fiends contrive terrible acts to destroy the world.

Subject to insatiable desire, drunk with hypocrisy and pride, holding false notions from delusion, they act with impure vows.

In their certainty that life consists in sating their desires, they suffer immeasurable anxiety that ends only with death.

Bound by a hundred fetters of hope, obsessed by desire and anger, they hoard wealth in stealthy ways to satisfy their desires.

"I have gained this wish today, and I shall attain that one; this wealth is mine, and there will be more.

I have killed that enemy, and I shall kill others too; I am the lord, I am the enjoyer, successful, strong, and happy.

I am wealthy, and wellborn, without peer, I shall sacrifice, give, rejoice."

So say men deluded by ignorance.

Confused by endless thoughts, caught in the net of delusion, given to satisfying their desires, they fall into hell's abyss.

Self-aggrandizing, stubborn, drunk with wealth and pride, they sacrifice in name only, in hypocrisy, violating all norms.

Submitting to individuality, power, arrogance, desire, and anger, they hate me and revile me in their own bodies, as in others.

These hateful, cruel, vile men of misfortune, I cast into demonic wombs through cycles of rebirth.

Fallen into a demonic womb, deluded in birth after birth, they fail to reach me, Arjuna, and they go the lowest way.

(Do we not see these conditions of ignorance on Earth fuelled by ignorance, desire, anger, and greed?

The three gates of hell that destroy the self are desire, anger, and greed; one must relinquish all three.

Released through these three gates of darkness, Arjuna, a man elevates the self and ascends to the highest way.

If he rejects norms of tradition and lives to fulfill his desires, he does not reach perfection or happiness or the highest way.

Let tradition be your standard in judging what to do or avoid; knowing the norms of tradition, perform your action here.

S. Threefold Nature of Faith.

Chapter Seventeen.

Arjuna: Men who ignore the ways of tradition but sacrifice in full faith, Krishna, what quality of nature is basic in them—lucidity, passion, or dark inertia?

Lord Krishna: Listen as I explain the threefold nature of faith inherent in the embodied self—lucid, passionate, and darkly inert.

The faith each man has, Arjuna, follows his degree of lucidity; a man consists of his faith, and as his faith is, so is he.

("For as a man thinketh in his heart, so is he." Proverbs 23:7)

Men of lucidity sacrifice to the gods; men of passion, to spirits and demons; the others, men of dark inertia, sacrifice to corpses and to ghosts.

Men who practice horrific penances that go against traditional norms are trapped in hypocrisy and individuality, overwhelmed by the emotion of desire.

Without reason, they torment the elements composing their bodies, and they torment me within them; know them to have demonic resolve.

Food is also of three kinds, to please each type of taste; sacrifice, penance, and charity likewise divide in three ways.

Foods that please lucid men are savory, smooth, firm, and rich; they promote long life, lucidity, strength, health, pleasure, and delight.

Passionate men crave foods that are bitter, sour, salty, hot, pungent, harsh, and burning, causing pain, grief, and sickness.

The food that please men of dark inertia is stale, unsavory, putrid, and spoiled, leavings unfit for sacrifice.

A sacrifice is offered with lucidity when the norms are kept and the mind is focused on the sacrificial act, without craving for its fruit.

But a sacrifice is offered with passion, Arjuna, when it is focused on the fruit and hypocrisy is at play.

A sacrifice is governed by dark inertia when it violates the norms—empty of faith, omitting the ritual offering of food and chants and gifts.

Honoring gods, priests, teachers, and wise men, being pure, honest, celibate, and nonviolent is called bodily penance.

Speaking truth without offense, giving comfort, and reciting sacred lore is called verbal penance.

Mental serenity, kindness, silence, self-restraint, and purity of being is called mental penance.

This threefold penance is lucid when men of discipline perform it with deep faith, without craving (an intense desire or longing) for reward.

Wavering and unstable, performed with hypocrisy, to gain respect, honor, and worship, that penance is called passionate.

Performed with deluded perception, self-mortification, or sadism, such penance has dark inertia.

Given in due time and place to a fit recipient who can give no advantage, charity is remembered as lucid.

But charity given reluctantly, to secure some service in return or to gain a future reward, is remembered as passionate.

Charity given out of place and time to an unfit recipient, ungraciously and with contempt, is remembered for its dark inertia.

OM TAT SAT: "That Is the Real"—this is the triple symbol of the infinite spirit that gave a primordial sanctity to priests, sacred lore, and sacrifice.

OM—knowers of the infinite spirit chant it as they perform acts of sacrifice, charity, and penance prescribed by tradition.

TAT—men who crave freedom utter it as they perform acts of sacrifice, charity, and penance, without concern for reward.

SAT—it means what is real and what is good, Arjuna; the word SAT is also used when an action merits praise.

SAT is steadfastness in sacrifice, in penance, in charity; any action of this order is denoted by SAT.

But oblation, charity, and penance offered without faith are called ASAT, for they have no reality here or in the world after death.

T. One With Infinite Spirit.

Chapter Eighteen.

Arjuna: Krishna, I want to know the real essence of both renunciation and relinquishment.

Lord Krishna: Giving up actions based on desire, the poets know as "renunciation"; relinquishing all fruit of action, learned men call "relinquishment."

Some wise men say all action is flawed and must be relinquished; others say action in sacrifice, charity, and penance must not be relinquished.

Arjuna, hear my decision about relinquishment; it is rightly declared to be of three kinds.

Actions in sacrifice, charity, and penance is to be performed, not relinquished—for wise men, they are acts of sanctity (holiness, saintliness, or godliness).

But even these actions should be done by relinquishing to me attachment and the fruit of action—this is my decisive idea.

Renunciation of prescribed action is inappropriate; relinquished in delusion, it becomes a way of dark inertia.

When one passionately relinquishes difficult action from fear of bodily harm, he cannot win the fruit of relinquishment.

But if one performs prescribed action because it must be done, relinquishing attachment and the fruit, his relinquishment is a lucid act.

He does not disdain unskilled action nor cling to skilled action; in his lucidity the relinquisher is wise and his doubts are cut away.

A man burdened by his body cannot completely relinquish actions, but a relinquisher is defined as one who can relinquish the fruits.

The fruit of action haunts men in death if they fail to relinquish all forms, unwanted, wanted, and mixed— but not if men renounce them.

Arjuna, learn from me the five causes for the success of all actions as explained in philosophical analysis.

They are the material basis, the agent, the different instruments, various kinds of behavior, and finally fate, the fifth.

Whatever action one initiates through body, speech, and mind, be it proper or perverse, these five causes are present.

This being so, when a man of poor understanding and misjudgment sees himself as the only agent, he cannot be said to see.

When one is free of individuality and his understanding is untainted, even if he kills these people, he does not kill and is not bound.

Knowledge, its object, and its subject are the triple stimulus of action; instrument, act, and agent are the constituents of action.

Knowledge, action, agent are threefold, differentiated by qualities of nature; hear how this has been explained in the philosophical analysis of qualities.

Know that through lucid knowledge one sees in all creatures a single, unchanging existence, undivided within its divisions.

(Oneness.)

Know passionate knowledge as that which regards various distinct existences separately in all creatures.

(Separation.)

But knowledge that clings to a single thing as if it were the whole, limited, lacking a sense of reality, is known for its dark inertia.

(Delusion, ignorance.)

Action known for its lucidity is necessary, free of attachment, performed without attraction or hatred by one who seeks no fruit.

Action called passionate is performed with great effort by an individualist who seeks to satisfy his desires.

Action defined by dark inertia is undertaken in delusion, without concern for consequences, for death or violence, or for manhood.

An agent called pure has no attachment or individualism, is resolute and energetic, unchanged in failure and success.

An agent said to be passionate is anxious to gain the fruit of action, greedy, essentially violent, impure, subject to excitement and grief.

An agent defined by dark inertia is undisciplined, vulgar, stubborn, fraudulent, dishonest, lazy, depressed, and slow to act.

Listen as I tell you without reserve about understanding and resolve, each in three aspects, according to the qualities of nature.

In one who knows activity and rest, acts of right and wrong, bravery and fear, bondage and freedom, understanding is lucid.

When one fails to discern sacred duty from chaos, right acts from wrong, understanding is passionate.

When it thinks in perverse ways, is covered in darkness, imagining chaos to be sacred duty, understanding is darkly inert.

When it sustains acts of mind, breath, and senses through discipline without wavering, resolve is lucid.

When it sustains with attachment duty, desire, and wealth, craving their fruits, resolve is passionate.

When a fool cannot escape dreaming, fear, grief, depression, and intoxication, courage is darkly inert.

Arjuna, now hear about joy, the three ways of finding delight through practice that brings an end to suffering.

The joy of lucidity at first seems like poison but is in the end like ambrosia, from the calm of self-understanding.

The joy that is passionate at first seems like ambrosia when senses encounter sense objects, but in the end it is like poison.

The joy arising from sleep, laziness, and negligence, self-deluding from beginning to end, is said to be darkly inert.

There is no being on earth or among the gods in heaven free from the triad of qualities that are born of nature.

The actions of priests, warriors, commoners, and servants are apportioned by qualities born of their intrinsic being.

Tranquility, control, penance, purity, patience, and honesty, knowledge, judgment, and piety are intrinsic to the action of a priest.

Heroism, fiery energy, resolve, skill, refusal to retreat in battle, charity, and majesty in conduct are intrinsic to the action of a warrior.

Farming, herding cattle, and commerce are intrinsic to the action of a commoner; action that is essentially service is intrinsic to the servant.

Each one achieves success by focusing on his own action; hear how one finds success by focusing on his own action.

By his own action a man finds success, worshipping the source of all creatures' activity, the presence pervading all that is.

Better to do one's duty imperfectly than to do another man's well; doing action intrinsic to his being, a man avoids guilt.

Arjuna, a man should not relinquish action he is born to, even if it is flawed; all undertakings are marred by a flaw, as fire is obscured by smoke.

His understanding everywhere detached, the self mastered, longing gone, one finds through renunciation the supreme success beyond action.

Understand in summary from me how when he achieves success one attains the infinite spirit, the highest state of knowledge.

Armed with his purified understanding, subduing the self with resolve, relinquishing sensuous objects, avoiding attraction and hatred;

Observing solitude, barely eating, restraining speech, body, and mind; practicing discipline in meditation, cultivating dispassion;

Freeing himself from individuality, force, pride, desire, anger, acquisitiveness; unpossessive, tranquil, he is at one with the infinite spirit.

Being at one with the infinite spirit, serene in himself, he does not grieve or crave; impartial toward all creatures, he achieves supreme devotion to me.

Through devotion he discerns me, just who and how vast I really am; and knowing me in reality, he enters into my presence.

Always performing all actions, taking refuge in me, he attains through my grace the eternal place beyond change.

Through reason, renounce all works in me, focus on me; relying on the discipline of understanding, always keep me in your thought.

If I am in your thought, by my grace you will transcend all dangers; but if you are deafened by individuality, you will be lost.

Your resolve is futile (completely ineffective) if a sense of individuality makes you think, "I shall not fight"—nature will compel you to.

You are bound by your own action, intrinsic to your being, Arjuna; even against your will you must do what delusion now makes you refuse.

Arjuna, the lord resides in the heart of all creatures, making them reel magically, as if a machine moved them.

With your whole being, Arjuna, take refuge in him alone—from his grace you will attain the eternal place that is peace.

The knowledge I have taught is more arcane (known or understood by very few; mysterious; secret; obscure;

esoteric) than any mystery—consider it completely, then act as you choose.

Listen to my profound words, the deepest mystery of all, for you are precious to me and I tell you for your good.

Keep your mind on me, be my devotee, sacrificing, bow to me—you will come to me, I promise, for you are dear to me.

Relinquishing all sacred duties to me, make me your only refuge; do not grieve, for I shall free you from all evils.

You must not speak of this to one who is without penance and devotion, or who does not wish to hear, or who finds fault in me.

When he shares this deepest mystery with others devoted to me, giving me his total devotion, a man will come to me without doubt.

No mortal can perform service for me that I value more, and no other man on earth will be more dear to me than he is.

(We pray that your reading of The Bhagavad-Gita has blessed you.)

I judge the man who studies our dialogue on sacred duty to offer me sacrifice through sacrifice in knowledge.

If he listens in faith, finding no fault, a man is free and will attain the cherished worlds of those who act in virtue.

Arjuna, have you listened with your full powers of reason? Has the delusion of ignorance now been destroyed?

Arjuna: Krishna, my delusion is destroyed, and by your grace I have regained memory; I stand here, my doubt dispelled, ready to act on your words.

Sanjaya: As I heard this wondrous dialogue between Krishna and Arjuna, the man of great soul, the hair bristled on my flesh.

By grace of the epic poet Vyasa, I heard the mystery of supreme discipline recounted by Krishna himself, the lord of discipline incarnate.

O King, when I keep remembering this wondrous and holy dialogue between Krishna and Arjuna, I rejoice again and again.

In my memory I recall again and again Krishna's wondrous form—great is my amazement, King; I rejoice again and again.

Where Krishna is lord of discipline and Arjuna is the archer, there do fortune, victory, abundance, and morality exist, so I think.

Here The Bhagavad-Gita concludes.

One must say that this text is without a doubt divine and knowledge directly from the Creator/God.

The writer feels inadequate to deliver a comment on The Bhagavad-Gita that rises to the level of its absolute power, magnificent beauty and ultimate truth.

With the help of Creator/God and his endless wisdom contained in The Bhagavad-Gita there is no doubt that ignorance on this beautiful planet Earth will be destroyed through the knowledge of the infinite spirit.

U. God, Humanity, Oneness.

At this point we will take a look at the major religious groups on Earth. What we will find is that there are a lot of similar, overlapping philosophical concepts that run through these groups. We find it is time that all religious organizations get together and join the people of the planet in the spiritual evolution of oneness. One could say that the world's religions are individual facets on the spiritual diamond that is Creator/God.

Christianity. Begun in the 1st century in the Middle East there are 2 billion to 2.2 billion adherents. Christianity is based on the teachings and life of Jesus Christ. It is a monotheistic (the doctrine that there is one God) religion. Christians commonly refer to Jesus as the Christ or messiah. The traditional Christian belief is that Jesus is the son of God, fully human and fully divine and humanity's savior. Jesus' teachings, his sacrificial death, and his resurrection are called "the good news" or gospel. The gospel is the revelation of God's eternal victory over the forces of evil. All people are given the promise of deliverance and life eternal by God's divine grace.

"You shall not take vengeance or bear any grudge against the sons of your own people, but you shall Love your neighbor as yourself: I am the Lord." --Leviticus 19:18

"Hear, O Israel: The Lord our God is one Lord, and you shall Love the Lord your God with all your heart, and with all your soul, and with all your might." -- Deuteronomy 6:4

"And he (Jesus) said, "What comes out of a man is what defiles a man. For from within, out of the heart of man, come evil thoughts, fornication, theft, murder, adultery, coveting, wickedness, deceit, licentiousness, envy, slander, pride, foolishness. All these evil things come from within, and they defile a man." --Mark 7: 20-23

I then asked him (Jesus), "Lord, what of the souls of the people who do not know whose people they are? Where do they go? He (Jesus) responded, "In those people the artificial spirit has grown strong and they have gone astray. Their souls are burdened, drawn to wickedness, and cast into forgetfulness. When they come forth from the body, such a soul is given over to the powers created by the rulers, bound in chains, and cast into prison again. Around and around it goes until it manages to become free from forgetfulness through knowledge, and so, eventually, it becomes perfect and is saved" --Gnostic Gospel of Thomas

This passage from the Gospel of Thomas seems to point to the concept of reincarnation. Cast into prison again could perhaps mean the soul returns to the body (prison) for another incarnation. Once the soul attains knowledge it becomes perfect and is saved; it escapes the cycle of birth and rebirth or reincarnation.

The Gospel of Thomas is one many Gnostic texts found in Nag Hammadi, Egypt in 1945 that add to the knowledge of the life of Jesus. Besides the Gnostic texts found in 1945 there have been a number of books written which claim that between the age of twelve and twenty-nine Jesus travelled widely, including years spent in India learning from gurus and sages the spiritual knowledge of Hinduism and Buddhism.

One such book was written in 1890 by Nicolas Notovitch and titled, "The Unknown Life of Christ." There has been some debate about the life of Jesus between the ages of twelve and twenty-nine as there is no mention of this period of the life of Jesus in the Bible.

Christianity has the largest number of adherents and is the largest major religious group on Earth

Islam. Islam was founded in the Arabian Peninsula during the 7th century and there are between 1.6 billion and 1.7 billion adherents around the world. It is a monotheistic (the doctrine that there is one God) religion whose central teachings are from the Qur'an, a text believed by Muslims (adherents of Islam) to be the word of God. Central as well are the teachings and life of Muhammad, considered by Muslims to be the last prophet of God.

Muslims believe that God is one and that the purpose of existence is to Love and serve God. The belief of Muslims is that Islam is the universal and complete version of the first faith that was revealed before through Jesus, Moses, and Abraham whom Muslims consider prophets. They assert that previous revelations and messages have been partly altered or corrupted through time. Muslims believe that the Qur'an has not been altered and is the final revelation from God.

"They will enter the garden of bliss who have a true, pure, and merciful heart." --Muhammad

"Ye will not enter Paradise until ye have faith, and ye will not complete your faith until ye Love one another."--Muhammad

Islam teaches that there is forgiveness for those who repent. As wealth is seen as a "trust from God's bounty" the well-off are to give zakat or alms to the needy as one of the obligations of the religion.

Hinduism. Hinduism is the predominant religion of the Indian subcontinent and one of its indigenous religions. There are between 850 million and 1 billion adherents around the world. Hinduism includes a wide array of laws or "daily morality" based on karma, dharma and the traditions of society. There are a number of traditions under the banner of Hinduism. It is a grouping of many intellectual or philosophical points of view, as opposed to a rigid set of beliefs.

Hinduism is made up of many different traditions and has no one founder. Hinduism goes back to its roots in the Iron Age and is called the oldest living major religion in the world. Hindu texts are divided into Sruti (revealed) and Smitri (remembered). The texts discuss temple building, rituals, mythology, theology and philosophy. The major scriptures are the Vedas, Upanishads, Mahabharata, Ramayana, Bhagavad-Gita and Agamas.

The first Vice-President of India Sarvepalli Radhakrishnan said that Hinduism is not "just a faith" but is a joining of intuition and reason; Hinduism cannot be described in traditional religious terms but can only be experienced. Of all of the major world religions Hinduism is considered the most complex. The Supreme Court of India thought that: "Unlike other religions in the world, the Hindu religion does not claim any one prophet, it does not worship any one God, it

119

does not believe in any one philosophic concept, it does not follow any one act of religious rites or performances, in fact, it doesn't satisfy the traditional features of a religion or creed. It is a way of life and nothing more."

Hinduism accepts all beliefs and dismisses religious labels which would imply division. It believes the world is one family that deifies the one truth. Virtually all Hindus believe that the soul or spirit called the atman is eternal. Brahman (God, supreme spirit) and atman (self, soul) are ultimately indistinct. The goal in life is to realize this; Brahman and atman are identical. According to the Upanishads when one becomes aware that one's innermost core has an identity with Brahman that person reaches Moksha (liberation or freedom).

To achieve the spiritual goal Moksha or Nirvana sages have taught a variety of methods (yogas).

* Bhakti yoga (the path of Love and devotion)

* Karma yoga (the path of right action)

*Raja yoga (the path of meditation)

* Jnana yoga (the path of wisdom)

The Hindu discipline of yoga trains the consciousness for spiritual insight, health and tranquility.

Because divinity permeates all things Hindus practice ahimsa (non-violence) and respect for all life.

Buddhism. Buddhism was founded in India in the 4th century B.C. and has 400 million to 500 million adherents worldwide. It is based on the teachings of Siddhartha Gautama who is referred to as the Buddha which means "The Awakened One" in Sanskrit and Pali. There are a variety of traditions, practices, and beliefs in Buddhism. The Buddha lived and taught sometime between the 6th and 4th centuries B.C.

He is seen by Buddhists as an enlightened teacher who shared his insights in an effort to end suffering (dukkha) through the elimination of ignorance (avidya). Through the elimination of desire and craving, and the understanding of dependent origination one attains nirvana or the highest happiness.

There are two major branches of Buddhism: Theravada ("The School of the Elders") and Mahayana ("The Great Vehicle"). Buddhism is most popular in Asia but both branches are practiced around the world. Schools have various paths to liberation but two of the most important teachings are no-self and dependent origination. The Buddha, the dharma (the teachings), and the sangha (the community) are the Three Jewels of Buddhist practices and traditions and the foundations.

Samsara is the cycle of birth and death and Buddhists strive to end the involuntary cycle by eliminating craving and desire, following the methods of Buddha and those who came after him.

Karma (work, action) is the force that drives samsara, the cycle of suffering and rebirth. The doing of good deeds and the doing of bad actions produce "seeds" in the mind that bear fruit in this life or the next incarnation. Unwholesome actions and deeds are to be avoided while striving to take positive action and do good deeds. What is important is the intent a person has when taking action with their body, mind or thoughts. These all combine to bring about consequences or fruits; the law of cause and effect.

The Four Noble Truths explain the nature of suffering (dukkha) and how it can be overcome.

* The truth of dukkha

* The truth of the origin of dukkha

* The truth of the cessation of dukkha

* The truth of the path leading to the end of dukkha

The Noble Eightfold Path leads to the end of suffering. Right view, right intention, right speech, right action, right livelihood, right effort and right concentration are considered The Noble Eightfold Path of Buddhism.

The Buddha taught a kindness meditation called "The Four Immeasurables" that builds a good attitude toward all sentient beings.

* May all sentient beings have happiness and its causes,

* May all sentient beings be free of suffering and its causes,

* May all sentient beings never be separated from bliss without suffering,

* May all sentient beings be in equanimity, free of bias, attachment and anger.

Folk religions. Folk religions are outside of the totality of official religious practices and customs. There are hundreds of millions of people worldwide who practice some form of a folk religion. They are fusions of philosophies and cultures which have different forms of expression which see a varying degree of combinations of traditional religions and cultural beliefs and customs.

An example would be the mixture of African folk beliefs with Roman Catholicism which resulted in the practice of Vodun and Santeria, originated in Cuba and Brazil.

There are many other forms of folk religion with a similar fusion of folk culture and formal religion around the world.

Chinese Folk Religion. Chinese folk religion is a term used to describe the various ethnic religious traditions that have been influential in the lives of 30% of the people of China to the present time. Shenism describes Chinese folk religion which includes the worship of shens (archetypes, consciousness, awareness, spirits, deities) which can be ancestors, dragons, demigods and heroes of culture, national deities, clan deities and nature deities.

Chinese folk religion is at times categorized with Taoism as Taoism sprang from folk religion and Chinese philosophy. Taoism is a mystical philosophical system developed and evolved by Lao-tzu and Chuang-tzu, advocating a life of complete simplicity, naturalness and non-interference. Lao-tzu lived in the 6th century B.C. Tao is the basic, eternal principle of the universe that transcends reality and is the source of being, non-being, and change.

Chinese folk religion is one of the major religious traditions in the world.

"In times of war men, civilized in peace, turn from their higher to their lower nature. But triumph is not beautiful. He who thinks a triumph beautiful is one with a will to kill. The death of a multitude is cause for mourning. Conduct your triumph as a funeral." Lao-tzu

"To be constantly without desire is the way to have a vision of the mystery (of heaven and earth): For constantly to have desire is the means by which their limitations are seen." Lao-tzu

Shinto. Shintoism is the original spiritual tradition of the Japanese people. Its adherents number from 35 million to 65 million. Its basic tenet is to reconnect the present Japan and its ancient past. It is a set of practices that were first recorded in the history of the Kojiki and Nihon Shoki of the 8th century. The earliest writings of Japanese Shintoism contain folklore, mythology and history.

The word Shinto (Way of the Gods) means spiritual, philosophical path or study. Kami (or spirit) and people are not separate but share the world of existence along with its complexities. Shinto is a term that applies to public shrines which include sectarian organizations, historical monuments, harvest festivals, war memorials and other purposes.

It teaches that good and bad deeds affect one's peace of mind and good fortune. Bad deeds create a type of ritual impurity which must be cleansed with the practice of purification rites. These rites are called harae and are the basis of Shinto. They are performed on a daily, weekly, seasonal, lunar and annual time frame.

Shinto has been called the religion of Japan. It teaches that everything contains a kami (spirit, God, spiritual essence). It is believed by Shintoists that kami is the innate force of a supernatural nature that is above the actions of man in the realm of the sacred.

Sikhism. Sikhism was founded in India and has 25 million to 30 million followers. It is a monotheistic religion that was begun in the 15th century by Guru Nanak Dev who was followed by ten successive gurus. The last teaching is the holy scripture Guru Granth Sahib. The religion centers around what has traditionally been known as the Gurmat or wisdom of the guru.

The principle Sikhi beliefs are faith in waheguru known by the phrase Ik Oankar which means one God. Included is the practice of the Sikh pursuing justice for all human beings in the area of social reform. Sikhs must learn to control internal vices and practice the virtues described in the Guru Granth Sahib.

The search for salvation is applied in congregational meditation on the message and name of God. Sikhi follow the teachings of the ten Sikh gurus (enlightened leaders) and the scriptural text the Guru Granth Sahib. They also follow the writings of six of the ten gurus as well as selected writings from devotees of various economic and religious backgrounds.

Sikhi traditions and teachings are resonant to the culture, society and history of Punjab, India where most Sikhs reside. Guru Nanak sums up the Sikh teaching: "Realization of truth is higher than all else. Higher still is truthful living."

Sikh teachings include the basic principle that all human beings are equal. They believe there should be no form of discrimination whether of creed, caste, or gender. Sikhs believe that no matter what religion, sex, or race one is, that all are equal in God's eyes.

To Sikhs God is sightless, shapeless, and timeless; infinite in power over everything and omnipresent. Guru Nanak describes how although God is not fully understandable by human beings, God is not wholly unknowable. God is in all creation and can be seen everywhere by those who are spiritually awakened. He places importance on the fact that God must be seen with "the inward eye" or the "heart" of human beings. Guru Nanak advised that through meditation one can realize communication with God.

Our ego is the biggest obstacle to our connection with God and truth. As our reconnection with truth is the supreme purpose of life, our honest meditation allows us to end the ego and gain truth and communication with God. Truth is a form of matter which is inside the body but is beyond time and death. When truth is accessed and allowed to shine in a person's heart, the wisdom of all holy texts of every religion are then understood by that person.

Judaism. Judaism was founded in the Levant region or the Middle East and has 15 million to 20 million adherents. It is the religion, philosophy and way of life of the Jewish people. Judaism is seen by religious Jews to be the lawful relationship of the children of Israel and God. It is a monotheistic religion begun from the Hebrew bible and articulated in later texts like the Talmud.

Rabbinic Judaism believes that God's commandments and laws were revealed on Mount Sinai to Moses in the written and oral Torah.

There are three movements included in Judaism and they are orthodox, conservation and reform. The difference among the three is their various interpretations of Jewish law. The orthodox believe that Jewish laws and the Torah are of divine origin and are eternal, therefore to be strictly adhered to. Conservatives and reformers have a more liberal view with conservatives holding a more traditional view than liberals. Liberal views hold that Jewish law should be seen as general guidelines without restrictive, obligatory observance which would be required of all Jews.

The core tenets of Judaism include Maimonides "Thirteen Principles of Faith". The first of the thirteen is "I believe in perfect faith that the Creator, blessed be his name, is the Creator and guide of everything that has been created; he alone has made, does make, and will make all things."

Jewish practices are typically understood through human values of self-respect, humility, compassion, loving-kindness, peace, truth and justice. Of central importance to Judaism is the sacred act of study of the Torah.

Jainism. Jainism was founded in India in the 9th century B.C. and has 9 million to 12 million followers. It is an Indian religion that emphasizes non-violence toward all living things. Jainism has a philosophy and practices that stress the necessity of self-effort to bring the soul to divine consciousness and liberation. All souls that have defeated their inner enemies and come to realize a state of supreme being are called jins or conquerors or victors.

The highest status of perfected souls is called siddha or one who has attained perfection or bliss. Jainism is referred to in the ancient texts as shraman dharma (self-reliant) and the "path of the Nirg Anthas" (those without attachments or aversions).The doctrine teaches that Jainism has always existed and will always be in existence.

Ratnatraya (triple jewels of Jainism) contains the path to liberation and are essential to Jain life. With the triple jewels one is able to move higher in spirituality.

* Right view (samyak darshan)

* Right knowledge (samyak gyana)

* Right conduct (samyak charitra)

Tattva are seven fundamentals which explain the nature of, and the solution to, the human predicament. Jain metaphysics are based on tattva.

* Soul (jiva): Perception, knowledge and consciousness make up the substance called soul.

* Non-soul (ajiva): Space, time and matter make up the non-soul.

* Influx (asrava): There is a flux of karmic matter that clings to the soul as a result of interaction between the soul and non-soul.

* Bondage (bandha): The potential of the soul to attain perfect knowledge and liberation is blocked due to the karmic matter that the soul accumulates.

* Stoppage (samvara): One can stop the accumulation of additional karmic matter through right conduct, right knowledge and right view.

* Dissociation (nirjara): It is possible to destroy existing karmic matter on the soul through asceticism.

* Liberation (moksha): Those souls which have destroyed their karmic matter are said to be liberated. Those souls have attained the pure quality of perfect knowledge in its true form.

One important doctrine of Jainism is anekantavada which refers to the fact that reality and truth are perceived differently from a diversity of viewpoints. It considers the views of all parties as there is no single point of view that is completely true.

Jain teachers teach that there are numerous ways that karmic matter can be attracted to the soul. Even if one is far away from acts of violence, karmic consequences will result from silent assent or endorsement of such violence. Jain scriptures advise great care when taking actions, an awareness of the world, and purity in the thoughts to avoid karmic matter and its oppressive weight.

Swami Vivekananda gave great credit to Jainism for its effects on Indian culture. He said about Jainism:

"What could have saved Indian society from the ponderous burden of omnifarious (of all varieties and kinds) ritualistic ceremonialism, with its animal and other sacrifices, which all but crushed the very life of it, except the Jain revolution, which took its strong stand exclusively on chaste morals and philosophical truths? Jains were the first great ascetics and they did some great work. "Don't injure and do good to all that you can, and that is all the morality and ethics, and that is all the work there is, and the rest is nonsense." All that we call ethics they simply bring out from that one great principle of non-injury and doing good."

Baha'i Faith. The Baha'i faith is a monotheistic religion which was founded in Iran in the 19th century. It has 7 million to 8 million estimated adherents. It was founded by Baha'u'llah in Persia (today known as Iran) and emphasizes the unity of all mankind. In the faith history, in religious and spiritual terms, is seen to be continually unfolding with a series of divine messengers who are appropriate for the time. These messengers are appropriate for the time and also according to the capacity of humanity of that time.

These messengers have included Jesus, Muhammad, Moses, Buddha and others. For the followers of Baha'i the most recent messengers have been Bab and Baha'u'llah. Those of the Baha'i faith believe the each consecutive messenger prophesied the messengers to follow. Baha'u'llah's life and teachings signified the end-times promises of previous scripture.

Humanity is seen to be in the process of collective evolution. The needs of the present time call for the establishment of global peace, unity and justice. The Baha'i faith teachings say that the purpose of life is to take the actions of service to mankind, reflection and prayer in order to learn to know and Love God.

The founders and central figures of most of the world's religions are seen as manifestations of God. The world's religions are accepted as valid as a result of the Baha'i belief in the progressive religious revelation of humanity.

Heaven and hell are seen to be spiritual states where there is either nearness or separation from God. These are states which describe our relationship with God in this world and the next; they are not physical places of reward or punishment. The unification of mankind is the highest concern in the political and religious conditions of the present world.

"I know now that there is no one thing that is true... It is all true." ~Ernest Hemingway

Oneness.

Perhaps Hemingway was articulating, whether he was consciously aware of it or not, oneness. Hemingway also said, "There is nothing to writing. All you do is sit down at a typewriter and bleed." Given all of the magnificent works of literature that have been created by men and women throughout human history there is the perennial effort by mankind to find a better way of living.

Through the use of words to convey thoughts, ideas and emotions mankind has seen the creation of artistic works of extraordinarily profound depth and wisdom. Even more profound knowledge is available in the great spiritual texts of the world. One would observe that it is not only artists and those who search for spiritual truth who are longing for the arrival at a point of truly understanding the meaning of life.

Every man, woman and child who walks this Earth in the year 2013 is longing for this true understanding.

2013 will be the time where every human being on Earth gains the true understanding of Unconditional

Love. That place inside of everything animate and inanimate which is of the Creator/God will be found by humanity. All will find that place inside where the truth resides. At that point there will be a collective grasp of the spiritual truths given by all of the great artists and spiritual masters who ever walked this beautiful planet Earth.

It is impossible for there not to be profound positive consequences for humanity as a result of this phenomenal increase of spiritual enlightenment. Our vision of the state of life on Earth in 2013 is constrained because we as humans will be experiencing the new, higher levels of spiritual knowledge on a scale that has never occurred on this planet.

Perhaps one would visualize the ideal world and this is what life on Earth will literally evolve to. The actual events and conditions on the ground of this planet will conform to the constituent elements that make up the substance of Unconditional Love. The state of affairs on Earth will be altered through the application of the most powerful force in the universe which is Love.

Creation is constantly occurring and what we see humanity creating at this time is a movement toward Heaven on Earth. Through the knowledge attained from our reconnection to Creator/God that is in all things there is no other road to travel but the road to oneness. As humanity now realizes that everyone and everything is of Creator/God the vision is undeniable. It is inevitable that life on this beautiful planet Earth will be transformed to mirror humanity's collective vision. The combination of every wish, every longing and every prayer for an ideal world held by every man, woman and child will be actualized into reality.

Oneness will be the condition in this world because oneness is what every human being wants in their heart. The infinite power of Unconditional Love will be the foundation of Earthly life because this is the prayer in the heart of all creatures in the universe. This is the path that all want to travel and so it is.

At the very core of the heart of all things there is the urge to experience Unconditional Love as it is the only reality. As this experiencing is the will of Creator/God it is also the will of humanity.

The Guru Granth Sahib. We conclude this work with verses from the Sikh spiritual text The Guru Granth Sahib.

Max Arthur Macauliffe (1841-1913) was a British administrator, prolific scholar and author. His relationship with the Sikh community resulted in his well known translations of Sikh scripture and history into English. He said the following about The Guru Granth Sahib.

"The Sikh religion differs as regards the authenticity of its dogmas from most other theological systems. Many of the great teachers the world has known have not left a line of their own composition and we only know what they taught through tradition or second-hand information. If Pythagoras wrote of his tenets, his writings have not descended to us. We know the teachings of Socrates only through the writings of Plato and Xenophon. Buddha has left no written memorial of his teaching. Confucius left no documents in which he detailed the principles of his moral and social system. The founder of Christianity did not reduce his doctrines to writing and for them we are obliged to trust the gospels of Matthew, Mark, Luke and John. The prophet Muhammad did not himself reduce to writing the chapters of the Qur'an. They were written or compiled by his adherents and followers. But the compositions of Sikh gurus are preserved and we know at firsthand what they taught."

Macauliffe believed The Guru Granth Sahib was matchless as a book of holy teachings.

Pearl Buck (1892-1973) was an American writer whose novel The Good Earth was the best selling fiction book in the United States in 1931 and 1932. Pearl Buck was awarded the Nobel Prize for Literature in 1938. She said the following about The Guru Granth Sahib after receiving its first English translation.

"I have studied the scriptures of the great religions, but I do not find elsewhere the same power of appeal to the heart and mind as I find here in these volumes. They are compact in spite of their length, and are a revelation of the vast reach of the human heart varying from the most noble concept of God, to the recognition and indeed the insistence upon the practical needs of the body. There is something strangely modern about the scriptures and this puzzles me until I learned that they are in fact comparatively modern, compiled as late as the 16th century, when explorers were beginning to discover that the globe upon which we all live is a single entity divided only by arbitrary lines of our own making. Perhaps this sense of unity is the source of power I find in these volumes. They speak to a person of any religion or of none. They speak for the human heart and the searching mind."

We pray that you will be profoundly blessed by the verses of Sapji Sahib from The Guru Granth Sahib.

Sapji Sahib, The Morning Prayer, contains the whole essence of Sikh philosophy.

Guru Nanak Dev was the founder of the religion of Sikhism in the 15th century and first in the line of ten Sikh Gurus.

There is one God.

God is from himself self-existent and self sufficient.

God was true in the beginning of creation.

God was true before the beginning of the ages.

God is true today.

Satguru Nanak says that he will prevail forever more.

Ritual purification though performed a million times may not purify the man's soul.

Even though one be silent and remains absorbed, silence of the mind is not obtained.

The hunger of the hungry who craves for more and more is appeased not, even if they possess the goods of the entire world.

Man may possess thousands and millions of clever tricks which shall not accompany the self to the next world.

How can we be true, and how can this screen of untruth be demolished?

Satguru Nanak says that the truth is realized through obedience to God's orders and will.

By the God's divine order all things came into being.

God's will cannot be expressed.

By God's divine orders all forms are being created and by his orders greatness is obtained.

By God's command the mortals are made high or low.

By God's command some are marked to be in grief and some are in happiness.

By his order some are blessed and some are made to whirl around in the circle of birth and death.

Everybody and everything is controlled by his command and none is exempted.

Satguru Nanak says that if one were to realize God's will one would never obtain egoism.

Those who are bestowed with power sing God's might.

Those who are blessed with gifts think of his blessings.

Some sing his virtues and the excellences of God.

Some worship him through learning and scholarship.

Some sing that he created beings and then reduces them to death.

Some sing that God takes away life and then gives it back.

Some sing that God seems distant and remote.

Some sing that God watches over us, face to face, ever present.

There is no shortage of persons who give discourses about God.

Millions upon millions discourse endlessly of God.

God goes on giving his gifts and recipients become tired of receiving.

Takers have been eating provisions throughout the ages.

He runs the universe by his commands.

Satguru Nanak says that the commander, the carefree one, is ever in bliss

God and his name are true.

True is his discipline and his language is of immense Love.

All creation begs of him for boons.

He goes on granting his gifts endlessly.

But what then can we offer to God so we may get a glimpse of his court?

What word should we utter so he can bestow his Love on us?

One must utter the divine name in the ambrosial hours early morning, and reflect upon God's greatness.

We obtain our body as a result of good deeds, but by God's grace we reach the gate of salvation.

Satguru Nanak says that one must realize that true God himself is all.

God is neither established nor created by anyone.

God is all in all himself. He himself is immaculate and pure.

Those who serve God obtain true honor.

Satguru Nanak advises that we sing God's praises who is the treasure of excellences.

Sing and hear God's praise and keep Love for him in your heart.

All one's grief is shed and one takes to their home joy and peace.

Guru's words are divine which infuse the knowledge of God and through guru's word God is realized to be all-pervading.

The God himself is Shiva, Vishnu, and Brahma and the goddesses like Parvati.

In other words God is destroyer, preserver and creator.

Even if I know his true greatness he cannot be described by words.

The guru has explained one thing to me.

There is but one creator of all creation and I should not forget him.

I should bathe at a place of pilgrimage only if it is acceptable to God. Without his approval it is of no use.

This universe is the creation of God and no one finds fulfillment without God's grace.

If we act upon and listen to the instructions of the guru then our mind enriches in invaluable qualities such as gems, jewels and rubies.

The guru has explained one thing to me.

There is but one creator of all creation and I should not forget him.

If someone lives the length of four ages and even ten times more, he becomes well known in all the nine continents and enjoys universal followings.

Though he would acquire a good name and obtain praise from all mankind, without God's grace no one will care for this person.

Even among worms he shall be treated as a worst worm and even the sinners impute accusations to him.

Satguru Nanak says that God grants virtues to the non-virtuous and bestows virtues on the virtuous.

There is none equal to him or shares his qualities.

By hearing the divine word of God, one becomes the perfect person, religious guide, spiritual hero and a great yogi.

By hearing the divine word of God, one can perceive the cosmic mysteries of the Earth, mythical bull and the sky.

By hearing the divine word of God, one can achieve the knowledge of continents, planets and nether regions.

By hearing the divine word of God, devotees become immune to death.

Satguru Nanak says that God's devotees always remain blissful.

By hearing the divine word of God, all the sufferings and sins are destroyed.

By hearing the divine word of God, status of gods like Shiva-god of death, Brahma-god of creation, Indra-god of rain is obtained.

By hearing the divine word of God, even sinners start praising God.

By hearing the divine word of God, one realizes the mysteries of the body and the way of uniting with God.

By hearing the divine word of God, knowledge of the four religious books, the six schools of philosophy and twenty-four ceremonial treatises is attained.

Satguru Nanak says that God's devotees always remain blissful.

By hearing the divine word of God truthfulness, divine knowledge and contentment is obtained.

Hearing the divine word of God equals bathing at the sixty-eight holy places of pilgrimage.

By hearing and reading again and again God's name, one gains true honor.

By hearing the divine word of God, one can fix the mind in meditating on the divine essence.

Satguru Nanak says that God's devotees always remain blissful.

By hearing the divine word of God, all the sufferings and sins are destroyed.

By hearing the divine word of God, one dives deep into the ocean of virtues.

Bt hearing the divine word of God, devotees become glorious like scholars, divines and kings.

By hearing the divine word of God, even the blind find the path.

By hearing the word of God, deep secrets of the oceans of truth are fathomed.

Satguru Nanak says that God's devotees always remain blissful.

By hearing the divine word of God, all the sufferings and sins are destroyed.

The state of the faithful cannot be described

If someone tries to describe it he shall later repent for impudence.

No paper, pen or writer can describe the believer's state, even though many may gather to ponder.

So immaculate is the divine word of God

It is realized if one worships him with full absorption of mind.

Through faith in God one can earn wisdom and consciousness.

By having complete faith the mind attains the knowledge of all the worlds.

Through faith one does not receive blows on the face.

Through faith one does not fear of death.

So immaculate is the divine word of God.

It is realized if one worships him with full absorption of mind.

Through faith in God, one shall meet no obstruction on the path of God's realization and departs with praise and honor.

Through faith in God one will move on the right path and not on the way of irrational belief.

The believer will develop his relationship toward virtue and righteousness.

Through faith and belief one can reach the door of salvation.

One also liberates those who are related to him.

Through faith and belief one establishes communion with God, and also liberates his followers by showing them the right path.

Satguru Nanak says that through faith one does not wander about begging for divine grace.

The saints are the ones affected by God, they are the elect supreme.

They are honored in God's court.

The saints are graced in the court of God.

They concentrate their minds on one guru alone.

One may attempt to express God's creation, one may try to describe him as much as possible, yet the doings of God are beyond count.

The mythical bull is dharma, the son and outcome of compassion.

It is patiently holding the Earth in order, whoever realizes this shall become a true man.

How much is the load on the bull!

There are many more and more earths, what power is that which supports their weight underneath?

Countless are creatures with their various names, kinds and colors.

The supreme God goes on writing them with his never ceasing pen.

Even if someone knows how to write this account, what a huge scroll of such writing it would be!

Who can calculate God's strength and the beautiful forms he has created and how can we judge the extent of his blessing?

With his one word all the creation came into being and millions of rivers began to flow.

O God how may I describe and express your might?

I am not worthy enough even once to be made a sacrifice to you.

Whatever pleases God is a good undertaking.

O God, you formless, eternal, without fear.

Innumerable are the persons who pray and admire God.

Innumerable are the forms of worship and modes of penance.

Countless are the scriptures and those who recite the Vedas.

Innumerable are the yogis who turn their minds away from the world.

Countless are the devotees reflecting on God's qualities and divine knowledge.

Countless are the pious mortals who distribute charities.

Countless are the spiritual heroes who bear the brunt on their faces in battle.

Countless are the devotees who in silence center their Love and attention on God.

Whatever pleases God is a good undertaking.

O God, you formless, eternal, without fear.

Countless are the fools who are spiritually blind.

Countless are the thieves and dishonest persons.

Countless are those who leave this world after establishing their kingdoms by force.

Countless are cut-throats who commit murders.

Countless are the sinners who depart after committing their sins.

Countless are the liars who wander in falsehood.

Countless are the filthy sinners who eat filth as their ration.

Countless are the slanderers who carry loads of sins on their heads.

Satguru Nanak describes the state of the lowly. I am not worthy enough even once to be made a sacrifice to you.

The names of gods and spaces created by him are countless.

His realms are inaccessible and inscrutable.

147

Even to call them countless amounts to carrying loads of sins on one's head.

God's name and praises are expressed through words.

God's virtues and knowledge are sung through words.

Through words the hymns are written and spoken.

The destiny written on one's forehead is described through words.

God, who writes these destinies, there are no such letters on his forehead.

We get in our fortune what he orders.

He has created nothing but the manifestation of his name and spirit.

There is no place without God's name.

If hands, feet and other parts of the body become filthy, it can be washed with water.

If clothes get polluted with urine, they can be washed off with soap.

If soul and conscience become polluted by sins, it can only be purified by devotions to the divine word of God.

Virtue and vice do not come by mere words.

Often repeated actions are engraved in the mind, and govern one's future and destiny.

Whatever you sow, you shall reap.

Satguru Nanak says that by God's order a man moves in the cycle of transmigration.

Pilgrimage, penance, compassion and charity giving have as little significance as that of a sesame seed. By themselves they bring only an iota of merit.

One who listens, obeys, believes and Loves God's divine word from the core of his heart, he takes the purifying bath of the soul.

God has all virtues and noble qualities, but I have none.

Without virtues and noble qualities, true devotion and meditation cannot be performed.

I salute God who is himself Brahma the creator and whose form is the divine word.

He is true, beautiful and eternal in his mind.

What was the time, the hour, the moment, the date, the day?

What was the season and the month when the creation was created?

If pundits found the answer they would be recorded in their holy scriptures.

Nor do the Qazis know the time or they would have recording in Qur'an.

Neither yogis nor no one else has known of the dates, days, the season and month of the creation.

Only the creator who creates the world knows the answer.

How are we to express his greatness, praise him and to know him?

Satguru Nanak says that everyone pretends to have knowledge of God and each one thinks he is wiser than the other.

Great is the master, great is his name.

All that happens proceeds from him.

Satguru Nanak says that if someone thinks himself to be powerful he will not be honored in the next world.

There are hundreds of thousands of nether worlds and skies.

The scriptures say that people have grown weary of searching the limits of God.

The saints, the religious books of Jews, Muslims and Christians gives an account of 18,000 worlds but all in vain.

But God is the principle of all creation.

The account of God cannot be written, as a person himself dies while writing the account.

Satguru Nanak says that God is great and he himself knows his own self.

One may sing God's glory again and again yet one cannot comprehend him.

It is like the streams and rivers which fall into the ocean do not know its limits.

Kings whose kingdom is as big as an ocean, and wealth as large as mountains, they are not even equal to an ant whose mind is fixed on God.

God's qualities and their narrations are countless.

Countless are the works and gifts of God.

Countless are his sights and sounds.

Limits of motives in God's mind are unknown.

Limits of his creation are unknown.

Limits of this and the other end of God's creation are unknown.

Endless yearnings were made to find his limits, but his limits cannot be found.

No one knows his limits, the more we describe the more is felt to describe.

Great is the God and his seat is high and his name is supreme above all.

If anyone be as great, as high as God, then alone he would know God's extent.

God alone knows how great he is.

Satguru Nanak says that blessings come through his glance of grace.

God's countless blessings and bounties cannot be expressed or recorded.

He is a great giver and expects nothing in return.

Many men and warriors beg at his door, those are many and beyond computation.

Many spoil away themselves in doing evil.

Countless are those who repeatedly receive God's gifts, but then deny receiving them.

Many fools receive the God's gratitude.

Many endure pain, hunger and grief and are continuously beaten.

Even these are God's gifts.

By God's will liberation and emancipation from bondage can be attained.

No one can say anything in this.

If any fool tries to intervene he knows that he will receive many lashes on his face.

God himself knows everything and he himself gives everything.

Very few are they who acknowledge this.

He to whom God showers the gift of his praises, Satguru Nanak says that he becomes king of kings.

God's virtues and spiritual traits are priceless.

Worshippers of God and his dealers and his treasures are priceless.

The seekers who come to God are priceless and those who come to purchase his name and devotion are priceless.

Priceless is the devotion to God and union with him.

His divine justice and divine court are invaluable.

His scales and weights through which he judges one's actions are priceless.

His blessings, gifts and marks of approval are priceless.

His grace and command are priceless.

No one can assess the value of priceless God.

Those who continuously speak of God remain absorbed in God's Love.

Those who recite the Vedas and puranas express his greatness.

The literate person repeats his name and delivers discourses about him.

Brahmas and Indras remember and speak of God.

Shiva and those with enlightened souls remember and speak of God.

Buddhas created by God remember and speak of him.

Demons and gods remember and speak of him.

The demi-gods, the spiritual warriors, the silent person, and the servants speak of God.

Many have given descriptions of God and made attempts to describe him.

Many have repeatedly described God and then they leave this world.

If God were to create as many more, as he has already created, even then no one can describe his virtues.

God becomes as great as it pleases him.

Satguru Nanak says that God himself knows his greatness.

If someone claims that he can describe God, he is put down as the greatest fool out of all fools.

Which is that gate, and which is that mansion, where God sits and takes care of all creation?

Countless are the musical instruments being played there by countless musicians.

Endless are the instruments, the notes, the players who sing in many musical measures with their consorts in divine praise.

Air, water, fire and the god of justice sing God's praises at his door.

The recording angels who know how to write our deeds, and on the basis of those recorded accounts, the god of justice, who examines and administers justice, also sing praises of God.

Lord Shiva, Lord Brahma and goddess ever beautiful and adorned are singing your praises in a beautiful way.

Indra, king of angels seated on his throne with other gods sings the praise of God at his gate.

In the meditative mood the perfect person sings of God and the saints in their contemplation sing as well.

Men of courage and tolerance, poise and contentment sing of you, and the dauntless warrior also sings your praises.

Scholars, the readers of the Vedas of all the ages, together with seven seers are singing your praises.

Fairies, the enchanting beauties of heaven, Earth and nether worlds are singing God's praises.

Invaluable objects created by God along with the sixty-eight places of pilgrimage are singing your praises.

Great warriors and divine heroes and the four sources of creation sing God's praises.

The continents, worlds and solar systems created and installed by God sing his glories.

God's saints who are pleasing to God are singing your praises.

Satguru Nanak says that many more who cannot be recollected in the mind sing God's praises.

God is the true master and his glory is true.

He created the creation, always exists, and will exist forever.

He shall not depart when the creation shall depart.

God who fashioned the world in innumerable ways of various species, colors and kinds, created the creation.

He looks at his hand-work which is the proof of his greatness.

God does whatever pleases him and none may command him.

Satguru Nanak says that he is the king of kings and one should live subject to his command.

Wear the earrings of contentment, make modesty your begging bowl, and meditation the ashes you smear on your body.

Make your coat from the realization of your mortality and keep your body virgin and make faith in God your walking stick.

Make your brotherhood with all the highest sect of yogic order, and by conquering your mind conquer the world.

I salute God again and again.

God is primal, pure with unknown beginning, indestructible and remains the same through all the ages.

Make divine knowledge your diet, store mercy within your mind and listen to the divine eternal music that beats in every heart.

God himself is the supreme master, and miracles are useless and of little significance.

Union and separation regulate God's creation and mortals get their share according to their deeds.

I salute God again and again.

Unique God creating the creation appointed three disciples, one of these is Brahma the creator, the other is Vishnu who sustains it, and the third is Shiva who decides the fate of the mortals.

As it pleases him and as is his order he makes them walk.

The most wonderful thing is that God sees them but they cannot see him.

God's seat and his stores are in countless worlds created by him.

Everything is put there once and for all, enough forever.

Having created the creation God is beholding it.

Satguru Nanak says that the works of true God are true.

Instead of one tongue may I have hundreds of thousands and twenty times that, and with each tongue, over and over again I would repeat God's name.

This is the path of stages leading to the master ascending to make union with God.

By hearing such sound of the songs of heaven even the meanest worms would desire to compete.

Satguru Nanak says that God is obtained by his grace and false is the boasting of the false ones.

It is not in anyone's power to speak or to remain silent.

It is not in anyone's power to beg or to give.

The man has no power to live or to die.

The man has no power to acquire riches and kingdoms which stirs a big commotion in the mind.

It is beyond our power to gain understanding of divine knowledge and meditation.

It is not in our power to find the path of freedom from the bondage of life and death.

God who has the power, exercises it and beholds it.

Satguru Nanak says that none can be good or bad by his own strength.

God created nights, seasons, lunar days and weekdays.

God created wind, water, fire, and the nether lands.

In between these God established the Earth as home to practice truth and virtue.

God created different kinds of species with various colors and habits, such species have countless different names.

They are judged according to their deeds and actions.

The God himself is true and true in his court.

There the accepted saints look graceful.

The marks of blessing and mercy of God is poured upon all.

The good and bad of everyone are judged there.

Satguru Nanak says that true facts become known in his court, when you go home you will see this.

The above is the moral duty of the realm of righteousness

Now we narrate the working of the realm of knowledge

Countless are winds, waters, fires, Krishnas and Shivas.

There are countless Brahmas who are fashioning in various forms, colors and clothes.

There are a number of earths and mountains for doing various deeds, and there are innumerable lessons to be learned.

There are many Indras, suns and moons, galaxies and countries.

There are countless yogis, enlightened ones, and countless forms of goddesses.

There are countless gods, demons, saints, jewels and oceans.

There are countless sources of creation, languages and many dominions of kings.

Countless are the men of divine knowledge and countless the servants of God.

Satguru Nanak says that there is no end to God's bounds.

In the domain of knowledge, spiritual learning shines brightly.

There it produces endless delight, melodies, amusement and joys.

The language of reaching the realm of spiritual happiness is beautiful.

Unique beautiful forms having no parallel are finished there.

What is happening in that sphere cannot be described.

If anyone attempts to describe it they shall have to repent afterwards.

There inner consciousness, intellect, soul and understanding are molded.

There the genius of the pious persons and men of miracles is molded.

In the sphere of action and grace the spiritual power is the main force.

No one else can reside there but those blessed with the spiritual force.

The very powerful warriors and heroes reside there.

In them the might of the pervading God remains fulfilled.

Everyone is fully merged with God's admiration there.

Their forms of beauty are indescribable.

They never die nor are they created because God's name resides in their hearts.

The saints of various worlds reside there.

They cherish the holy eternal ever in their hearts.

Formless God resides in the realm of truth.

God beholds the creation which he has created, and grants his kind glance and bestows upon them happiness.

There are continents, universes and solar systems in that region.

If someone tries to describe them he knows there is no limit or end to this.

There are universe upon universe and creations over creations.

They function according to orders issued by God.

God beholds his creation and feels happy by contemplating over it.

Satguru Nanak says that to describe the realm of truth is as hard as steel.

Make purity and modesty your furnaces and patience as your goldsmith.

Consider your mind as your anvil and divine knowledge as your tools.

Consider fear of God is as your bellows and practice of penance is the fire.

Treat the Love of God as thought where in filters the nectar of God's name.

Thus in the true mint, the divine word is fashioned.

This is the daily routine of those on whom God casts his divine grace.

Satguru Nanak says that God with his kind look makes them happy.

Air is the guru, water is the father and Earth is the great mother.

Days and nights are the two nurses, in whose laps the whole world is at play. Good and bad deeds are judged by the God of justice.

According to their deeds, some will be adjusted near him and some will be distant from God.

Those who have contemplated his divine word would pass through all toils.

Satguru Nanak says that their faces flow with the glory of the divine light and many more are saved along with them.

Thank you for reading LOVE 2013.

****